Theological Resources for Ministry

A Bibliography of Works in Theological Studies

Don Thorsen

Evangel Publishing House
Nappanee, IN

ISBN: 0-916035-71-9

Library of Congress Catalog Card Number: 96-86314

Printed in the United States of America

5 4 3 2 1

This book is dedicated to my siblings

Judy, Carl and Norman

who all minister in distinctive ways

FOREWORD

This book will help readers to track down sources and information on numerous biblical and theological themes. It is well ordered and user-friendly. It is concise, objective, and not biased or tilted to particular opinions.

Beginning students in religious studies can go to its "Doctrine" section and find well-selected resources on key doctrinal topics. They can go to its "Theological Traditions" section and find an abundance of sources to describe various Christian traditions. They can go to its "Contemporary Theological Issues" section and find further literature on such important topics as ecology, civil religion, and violence.

Although this bibliography is limited largely to English sources or translations, it has carefully selected from the massive resources available those that the student will find most useful. Don Thorsen has rendered a useful service by providing such a succinct bibliography of crucial resources for theological and religious studies.

Thomas C. Oden

TABLE OF CONTENTS

Theological Traditions

Contemporary Theological Issues

Appendix

INTRODUCTION

Theology represents an integral part of ministry. Theology provides the theoretical background for all that we believe and practice as Christians. It has been said that nothing is as practical as a good theory. This practicality results from the fact that the best theories inform the best practice. Likewise, the best practice informs the best theories. So the availability of theological resources in a bibliography represents a valuable tool for anyone interested in ministry as well as issues of theology. A theological bibliography is especially valuable to those preparing for ministry because it provides a convenient resource for investigating theological issues in an in-depth way.

This bibliography serves as a complement to a previous work entitled *Biblical Resources for Ministry* written by David R. Bauer. The three considerations that served to determine selections for that bibliography are reflected here. Although this book contains more than two thousand titles by more than one thousand authors, it is still quite selective, containing only a portion of the books that could have been included. Inclusion of individual works was based upon one or more of the following considerations. First, books were chosen because of their usefulness for theological understanding within the broad context of the faith of the church. I chose books that are ancient and modern, eastern and western, catholic and protestant, conservative and liberal.

Second, books were chosen because of their significance in the history of Christian theology. This involves the selection of books that may not reflect my own theology or theology of the person investigating this bibliography. So the reader should think critically about each of the suggested readings.

Third, books were chosen because of their evangelical scholarship. This includes evangelical Wesleyan scholarship, which reflects my own theological background. This consideration, however, does not negate the previous two considerations. The ecumenical spirit of John Wesley's theology encourages rather than discourages a breadth of theological consideration, especially when reflecting upon issues related to ministry.

I marked with an asterisk (*) those books that I recommend most to readers. These special recommendations reflect the best of the three considerations listed above. I encourage readers to become aware of a breadth of knowledge rather than knowledge that is doctrinaire.

Certainly no two scholars would choose exactly the same books for inclusion in this bibliography or make the same special recommendations. My choices were a matter of individual judgment. So the reader should look upon the bibliography as suggestive rather than determinative of ways in which to begin one's own investigative work. Nothing takes the place of individual research and reflection upon theological issues that are of personal concern or that are of concern to ministry. Test the bibliography for its usefulness as a tool for your research.

Since this book was prepared primarily for ministers and those preparing for ministry, I tried to organize the bibliography in a straightforward way. For example, I included a wide variety of section headings. I only included works in English, though these works will direct you to further readings currently unavailable in the English language. Also, I only included that bibliographical information necessary for finding the works listed. I did not, however, include essentially homiletical or devotional volumes, not because they lack value as such, but because they stand outside the theological focus of this bibliography.

The bibliography should acquaint readers with major works, significant publishers, and prominent scholars in theological studies. It should also assist people in the development of their personal libraries. For example, I recommend that people acquire theological dictionaries that span a variety of theological backgrounds and disciplines. Theological dictionaries serve as a helpful starting point for research because they provide an overview of issues as well as suggest further readings and areas of study. Since most theological dictionaries reflect a particular way of viewing theology, the acquisition of a variety of them help to develop a broader and healthier approach to theological investigation.

The ultimate purpose of the bibliography is to direct readers to those works that will be most helpful in integrating theology and ministry. Similar to Bauer's *Biblical Resources for Ministry*, I have operated on the basis of a number of assumptions. First, theological investigation is foundational for both personal and ministry development and is therefore to be pursued with all seriousness.

Second, primary readings in theology are preferred over secondary readings, which tend to be more summative than constructive. Secondary readings can be very useful, but they should not take the place of original authors, especially those historic authors who provided the theological foundation on which contemporary authors stand. Sometimes in our concern for contemporary theological issues, we neglect the wealth of insight available to us throughout the whole of church history. Most of the works listed in this bibliography are relatively recent publications because of my concern to provide up-to-date theological information. But I have not neglected classical theological writings from historic Christian authors. In particular, I recommend that readers become familiar with the works of those found in the section on Notable Theologians.

Finally, I assume that there is value in encountering theology from different theological traditions as well as various periods in church history. While celebrating our participation in our own traditions, we should recognize that Christian theology and ministry is larger than the construals of individual faith communities. So our understanding can be enhanced by insights from those who represent theological commitments other than our own. It is within this context of dialogue that our theology and ministry best develops.

It is my hope that anyone with interests in Christian theology or ministry will benefit from *Theological Resources for Ministry*. Theology and ministry take place in many ways. This is why I dedicated the book to my siblings who uniquely minister to me as well as to others.

I would like to thank Gary Freymiller, Editor of Evangel Publishing House, whose vision for Christian scholarship and trust in me made this project possible. I would also like to thank Thomas Oden for his leadership in promoting bibliographical resources for ministry that emphasize the key texts of classical Christian consciousness. My section on Notable Theologians draws upon his work in *Agenda for Theology: Recovering Christian Roots* (San Francisco: Harper & Row, 1979). Next I would like to thank Scott Weiner, who diligently served as my assistant and did much of the preliminary research for the project, and Dale

Nelson, who assisted me in doing the index. Finally, I would like to thank the Research and Faculty Development Councils at Azusa Pacific University for providing the funding for my research assistants.

Don Thorsen
Azusa, California

THEOLOGICAL REFERENCE WORKS

Library and Research Guides

Your theological research will become more effective as you become familiar with library resources available to you.

Aldrich, Ella V. *Using Theological Books and Libraries*. Englewood Cliffs, NJ: Prentice-Hall, 1963.

*Badke, William B. *The Survivor's Guide to Library Research*. Grand Rapids: Zondervan, 1990.

Barber, Cyril J. *The Minister's Library*. Grand Rapids: Baker, 1974.

Bolich, Gregory G. *The Christian Scholar: An Introduction to Theological Research*. Lanham, MD: University Press of America, 1986.

Bollier, John A. *Tools for Continuing Self-Education: A Guide to Literature of Theology*. New Haven: Yale Divinity School Library, 1976.

Delivuk, John A. *How to Find Information in the Seminary Library*. St. Louis: Concordia Seminary Library, 1985.

Kennedy, James R. *Library Research Guide to Religion and Theology*. 2nd rev. ed. Ann Arbor: Pierian, 1984.

Kepple, Robert J. *Reference Works for Theological Research: An Annotated Selective Bibliographical Guide*. 2nd ed. Washington, DC: University Press of America, 1981.

*Krupp, Robert A. *A Primer on Theological Research Tools*. Lanham, MD: University Press of America, 1990.

*Mann, Thomas. *A Guide to Library Research Methods*. New York: Oxford University Press, 1987.

Sayre, John L., and Roberta Hamburger. *Tools for Theological Research*. 7th ed. Enid, OK: Seminary, 1985.

Southard, Samuel. *Religious Inquiry: An Introduction to the Why and How*. Nashville: Abingdon, 1976.

Tucker, Dennis C. *Finding Religion (in the Library): A Student Manual of Information Retrieval and Utilization Skills*. Bristol, IN: Wyndham Hall, 1989.

Bibliographies

The following bibliographical materials provide additional theological resources for your use.

Bauer, Gerhard. *Towards a Theology of Development: An Annotated Bibliography*. Geneva: Ecumenical Centre, 1970.

*Bollier, John A. *The Literature of Theology: A Guide for Students and Pastors*. Philadelphia: Westminster, 1979.

Branson, Mark L. *The Reader's Guide to the Best Evangelical Books*. San Francisco: Harper & Row, 1982.

*Davis, John J. *Theology Primer: Resources for the Theological Student*. Grand Rapids: Baker, 1981.

Fraker, Anne T., ed. *Religion and American Life: Resources*. Urbana: University of Illinois Press, 1989.

Freudenberger, Elsie. *Reference Works in the Field of Religion: A Selective Bibliography*. Haverford, PA: Catholic Library Association, 1986.

Gorman, G.E., et al. 3 vols. *Theological and Religious Reference Materials*. Westport, CT: Greenwood, 1984-1986.

*Kepple, Robert J., and John R. Muether. *Reference Works for Theological Research: An Annotated Selective Bibliographical Guide*. 3rd ed. New York: University Press of America, 1991.

Religious Books, 1876-1982. 4 vols. Prepared by the R.R. Bowker Company's Department of Bibliography in collaboration with the Publications Systems Department. New York: Bowker, 1983.

Indexes and Abstracts

There are hundreds of theological journals, magazines, abstracts and other sources of theology. Rather than list them all, only indexes and abstracts have been listed. However, these reference materials provide excellent resources for doing theological research in almost every area of life. The indexes and abstracts can be found in most theological libraries.

**ATLA Religion Indexes* (CD-ROM).

Dissertation Abstracts (Available through *First Search*. See librarian.)

New Testament Abstracts.

Old Testament Abstracts.

Reader's Guide to Periodical Literature.

**Religion Index One.* (Index of religious literature. Included in the ATLA Religion Index on CD-ROM.)

**Religion Index Two.* (Index of multi-author religious works. Included in the ATLA Religion Index on CD-ROM.)

**Research in Ministry.*

The Review of Books in Religion.

Theological Book Review.

Theological Dictionaries

Theological dictionaries represent one of the most useful tools for studying any Christian belief. They provide brief explanations along with historical background and bibliographical references for further study.

Angeles, Peter A. *Dictionary of Christian Theology*. San Francisco: Harper & Row, 1985.

Burgess, Stanley M., and Gary B. McGee, eds. *Dictionary of Pentecostal and Charismatic Movements*. Grand Rapids: Zondervan, 1988.

Cohn-Sherbok, Dan. *A Dictionary of Judaism and Christianity*. Philadelphia: Trinity Press International, 1991.

*Elwell, Walter A., ed. *Evangelical Dictionary of Theology*. Grand Rapids: Baker, 1984.

*Ferguson, Sinclair B., et al, eds. *New Dictionary of Theology*. Downers Grove: InterVarsity, 1988.

Gentz, William H., ed. *The Dictionary of Bible and Religion*. Nashville: Abingdon, 1986.

Hardon, John A. *Pocket Catholic Dictionary*. New York: Doubleday, 1985.

Harrison, Everett F., ed. *Baker's Dictionary of Theology*. Grand Rapids: Baker, 1985.

*Komonchak, Joseph, et al, eds. *The New Dictionary of Theology*. Collegeville, MN: Liturgical, 1987.

*Livingstone, Elizabeth A., ed. *The Concise Oxford Dictionary of the Christian Church*. New York: Oxford University Press, 1980.

Mather, George, and Larry A. Nichols. *Dictionary of Cults, Sects, Religions and the Occult*. Grand Rapids: Zondervan, 1993.

Miethe, Terry, L., ed. *The Compact Dictionary of Doctrinal Words*. Minneapolis: Bethany House, 1988.

*Musser, Donald W., and Joseph L. Price, eds. *A New Handbook of Christian Theology*. Nashville: Abingdon, 1992.

Rahner, Karl. *Concise Theological Dictionary*. London: Burns & Oates, 1983.

Rahner, Karl, and Herbert Vorgrimler. *Concise Theological Dictionary*. 2nd ed. London: Burns & Oates, 1983.

Richardson, Alan, and John Bowden, eds. *The Westminster Dictionary of Christian Theology*. Philadelphia: Westminster, 1983.

Taylor, Richard S., et al., eds. *Beacon Dictionary of Theology*. Kansas City: Beacon Hill, 1984.

Wakefield, Gordon. S., ed. *A Dictionary of Christian Spirituality*. Philadelphia: Westminster, 1983.

Theological Encyclopedias

Theological encyclopedias usually provide more in-depth information about Christian beliefs than a theological dictionary. An encyclopedia provides a broad discussion of theological issues.

*Catholic University of America. *The New Catholic Encyclopedia*. 18 vols. New York: McGraw-Hill, 1967.

Glazier, Michael, and Monika K. Hellwig, eds. *The Modern Catholic Encyclopedia*. Collegeville, MN: Liturgical, 1994.

McBrien, Richard P., ed. *The HarperCollins Encyclopedia of Catholicism*. San Francisco: HarperSanFrancisco, 1995.

McClintock, John, and James Strong. *Cyclopedia of Biblical, Theological, and Ecclesiastical Literature*. 12 vols. Grand Rapids: Baker, 1981.

*McGrath, Alister E., ed. *The Blackwell Encyclopedia of Modern Christian Thought*. Oxford: Blackwell, 1993.

Rahner, Karl, ed. *Encyclopedia of Theology: The Concise Sacramentum Mundi*. Rev., abr. ed. New York: Crossroad, 1975.

Dictionaries of Religion

Dictionaries of religion present more of an inter-religious approach to theological issues.

*Adams, Hannah. *A Dictionary of All Religions and Religious Denominations: Jewish, Heathen, Mahometan, Christian, Ancient, and Modern*. Atlanta: Scholars, 1992.

Cohn-Sherbok, Dan. *A Dictionary of Judaism and Christianity*. Philadelphia: Trinity Press International, 1991.

*Hexham, Irving. *Concise Dictionary of Religion*. Downers Grove: InterVarsity, 1993.

MacGregor, Geddes. *Dictionary of Religion and Philosophy*. New York: Paragon House, 1991.

*Meagher, Paul K., et al. *The Encyclopedic Dictionary of Religion*. 3 vols. Washington: Catholic University Press, 1979.

Reese, William L. *Dictionary of Philosophy and Religion: Eastern and Western Thought*. Atlantic Highlands, NJ: Humanities, 1980.

Smith, Jonathan Z., ed. *The Harper Collins Dictionary of Religion*. San Francisco: HarperCollins, 1995.

Encyclopedias of Religion

Encyclopedias of religion provide a broad inter-religious approach to the discussion of theological issues, which sometimes include comparative religious studies.

Barrett, David, ed. *World Christian Encyclopedia: A Comparative Survey of Churches and Religions in the Modern World*. New York: Oxford University Press, 1982.

Beit-Hallahmi, Benjamin. *The Illustrated Encyclopedia of Active New Religions, Sects, and Cults*. New York: Rosen, 1993.

*Douglas, James D., ed. *New Twentieth-Century Encyclopedia of Religious Knowledge*. Rev. ed. Grand Rapids: Baker, 1991.

*Eliade, Mircea, ed. *Encyclopedia of Religion*. 16 vols. New York: Macmillan, 1986.

Encyclopaedia Judaica Research Foundation. *Encyclopaedia Judaica*. 18 vols. Jerusalem: Encyclopaedia Judaica, 1972-1982.

Guiley, Rosemary E., ed. *Harper's Encyclopedia of Mystical and Paranormal Experience*. San Francisco: HarperSanFrancisco, 1991.

Hastings, James, ed. *The Encyclopedia of Religion and Ethics*. 13 vols. New York: Scribner's, 1979-1980, [1910]-1934.

Murphy, Larry G., et al., eds. *Encyclopedia of African American Religions*. New York: Garland, 1993.

Introductions to Theology (Single-Volume)

(See also Notable Theologians)

Ashcroft, Morris. *Christian Faith and Beliefs*. Nashville: Broadman & Holman, 1984.

Berkhof, Hendrikus. *Christian Faith: An Introduction to the Study of the Faith*. Rev. ed. Grand Rapids: Eerdmans, 1986.

Berkhof, Louis. *Systematic Theology*. 3rd ed. Grand Rapids: Eerdmans, 1946.

Boice, James M. *Foundations of the Christian Faith*. Rev. ed. Downers Grove: InterVarsity, 1986.

Braaten, Carl E., and Robert W. Jenson, eds. *Christian Dogmatics*. Philadelphia: Fortress, 1984.

Conyers, A.J. *A Basic Christian Theology*. Nashville: Broadman & Holman, 1995.

*Erickson, Millard J. *Introducing Christian Doctrine*. Grand Rapids: Baker, 1992.

Fackre, Gabriel J. *The Christian Story*. Grand Rapids: Eerdmans, 1984.

Grenz, Stanley J. *Theology for the Community of God*. Nashville: Broadman & Holman, 1994.

Grudem, Wayne A. *Systematic Theology: An Introduction to Christian Doctrine*. Grand Rapids: Zondervan, 1994.

*Guthrie, Jr., Shirley. *Christian Doctrine*. Rev. ed. Louisville: Westminster/John Knox, 1994.

*Hodgson, Peter C., and Robert H. King, eds. *Christian Theology: An Introduction to Its Traditions and Tasks*. 2nd ed. Minneapolis: Fortress, 1994.

Holmes, Urban T. *To Speak of God*. New York: Seabury, 1974.

*Johnson, Alan F., and Robert Webber. *What Christians Believe: A Biblical and Historical Summary*. Grand Rapids: Zondervan, 1989.

Küng, Hans. *Theology for the Third Millennium: An Ecumenical View*. New York: Doubleday, 1988.

Leith, John H. *Basic Christian Doctrine*. Louisville: Westminster/John Knox, 1993.

*McGrath, Alister E. *Christian Theology: An Introduction*. Cambridge, MA: Blackwell, 1994.

Migliore, Daniel L. *Faith Seeking Understanding: An Introduction to Christian Theology*. Grand Rapids: Eerdmans, 1991.

*Pannenberg, Wolfhart. *An Introduction to Systematic Theology*. Grand Rapids: Eerdmans, 1991.

Purkiser, W.T. *Exploring Our Christian Faith*. Kansas City: Beacon Hill, 1960.

Rahner, Karl. *Foundations of Christian Faith*. New York: Seabury, 1978.

Thiessen, Henry C. *Lectures in Systematic Theology*. Grand Rapids: Eerdmans, 1979.

TYPES OF THEOLOGY

There are various ways to classify the different types of theology. The following classification represents an introduction to traditional ways in which the study of theology has been sub-divided.

Biblical Theology

Biblical theology represents the breadth of theology as it arises out of a study of the biblical text in its original context. Emphasis is placed upon biblical theologies that cover the whole of scripture.

(See also Bible)

Ackroyd, Peter R., et. al., eds. *The Cambridge History of the Bible*. 3 vols. Cambridge: University Press, 1963-1970.

Bauer, Johannes B., ed. *Encyclopedia of Biblical Theology: The Complete Sacramentum Verbi*. Rev. ed. New York: Crossroad, 1981.

*Bright, John. *The Kingdom of God*. Nashville: Abingdon, 1953.

Burrows, Millar. *An Outline of Biblical Theology*. Philadelphia: Westminster, 1946.

*Childs, Brevard S. *Biblical Theology in Crisis*. Philadelphia: Fortress, 1970.

——. *Biblical Theology of the Old and New Testaments: Theological Reflection on the Christian Bible*. Minneapolis: Fortress, 1993.

*Cullmann, Oscar. *Salvation in History*. New York: Harper & Row, 1967.

Gerhardsson, Birger. *The Ethos of the Bible*. Philadelphia: Fortress, 1981.

*Léon-Dufour, Xavier, ed. *Dictionary of Biblical Theology*. 2nd ed. New York: Seabury, 1973.

Purkiser, W.T., et al. *God, Man, and Salvation: A Biblical Theology*. Kansas City: Beacon Hill, 1977.

*Reumann, John H.P., ed. *The Promise and Practice of Biblical Theology*. Philadelphia: Fortress, 1991.

Smart, James D. *The Past, Present, and Future of Biblical Theology*. Philadelphia: Westminster, 1979.

Stuhlmacher, Peter. *How to Do Biblical Theology*. Allison Park, PA: Pickwick, 1995.

Stuhlmueller, Carol, ed. *The Collegeville Pastoral Dictionary of Biblical Theology*. Collegeville, MN: Liturgical, 1994.

Vos, Geerhardus. *Biblical Theology: Old and New Testaments*. Grand Rapids: Eerdmans, 1948.

Historical Theology

Historical theology provides a historical investigation of theology as it developed in church history.

(See also History)

Berkhof, Louis. *The History of Christian Doctrines*. London: Banner of Truth, 1969.

*Berneking, Nancy J., and Pamela C. Joern, eds. *In Her Words: Women's Writings in the History of Christian Thought*. Nashville: Abingdon, 1994.

Braaten, Carl E., and Robert W. Jenson, eds. *A Map of Twentieth-Century Theology*. Minneapolis: Augsburg Fortress, 1995.

Congar, Yves. *A History of Theology*. Garden City, NY: Doubleday, 1968.

Forell, George W., ed. *Christian Social Teachings*. Minneapolis: Augsburg, 1971.

*Grenz, Stanley J., and Roger E. Olson. *20th-Century Theology*. Downers Grove: InterVarsity, 1992.

*Jordan, Mark D., ed. *Medieval Philosophy & Theology*. Vol 1-. Notre Dame: University of Notre Dame, 1991-.

Kaufman, Gordon D. *Systematic Theology: A Historicist Perspective*. New York: Scribner's, 1968.

*Leith, John H. *Basic Christian Doctrine: A Summary of Christian Faith - Catholic, Protestant, and Reformed*. Louisville: Westminster/John Knox, 1992.

*Livingstone, Elizabeth A., ed. *The Concise Oxford Dictionary of the Christian Church*. New York: Oxford University Press, 1980.

Lohse, Bernhard. *A Short History of Christian Doctrine*. Philadelphia: Fortress, 1966.

Mackintosh, H. R. *Types of Modern Theology: Schleiermacher to Barth*. London: Nisbet, 1937.

Macquarrie, John. *Twentieth Century Religious Thought*. New York: Scribner's, 1981.

McKim, Donald K. *Theological Turning Points: Major Issues in Christian Thought*. Louisville: Westminster/John Knox, 1989.

Muller, Richard A. *Latin and Greek Theological Terms*. Grand Rapids: Baker, 1985.

Niesel, Wilhelm. *Reformed Symbolics: A Comparison of Catholicism, Orthodoxy and Protestantism*. Edinburgh: Oliver and Boyd, 1962.

*Pelikan, Jaroslav J. *The Christian Tradition: A History of the Development of Doctrine*. 5 vols. Chicago: University of Chicago Press, 1971-1989.

*——. *From Luther to Kierkegaard: A Study in the History of Theology*. St. Louis: Concordia, 1963.

*Pelikan, Jaroslav J. *Twentieth Century Theology in the Making*. 3 vols. London: Fontana, 1970.

Ricoeur, Paul. *The Reality of the Historical Past*. Milwaukee: Marquette, 1984.

Sykes, Stephen W. *The Identity of Christianity*. Philadelphia: Fortress, 1984.

Troeltsch, Ernst. *The Christian Faith*. Minneapolis: Augsburg Fortress, 1991.

Urban, Linwood. *A Shorter History of Christian Thought*. Rev. ed. New York: Oxford University Press, 1995.

Wilken, Robert L. *Remembering the Christian Past*. Grand Rapids: Eerdmans, 1995.

Wood, Charles M. *The Formation of Christian Understanding*. Philadelphia: Westminster, 1981.

Moral Theology (Ethics)

Moral theology represents the study of right and wrong in moral behavior or what is good for people. Protestants usually refer to this study as *ethics*, whereas Roman Catholics refer to it as *moral theology*.

Anderson, James N.D. *Morality, Law and Grace*. London: Tyndale, 1972.

Baier, Kurt. *The Moral Point of View*. Ithaca, NY: Cornell University Press, 1958.

*Beach, Waldo, and H. Richard Niebuhr, eds. *Christian Ethics: Sources of the Living Tradition*. New York: Ronald, 1955.

*Bonhoeffer, Dietrich. *Ethics*. London: SCM, 1955.

Chiba, Shin, et al., eds. *Christian Ethics in Ecumenical Context: Theology, Culture, and Politics in Dialogue*. Grand Rapids: Eerdmans, 1995.

Curran, Charles E. *Toward an American Catholic Moral Theology*. Notre Dame: University of Notre Dame Press, 1987.

Daly, Lois K., ed. *Feminist Theological Ethics: A Reader*. Louisville: Westminster/John Knox, 1994.

Finnis, John. *Natural Law and Natural Rights*. New York: Oxford University Press, 1980.

Fletcher, Joseph F. *Situation Ethics: The New Morality*. Philadelphia: Westminster, 1966.

Geisler, Norman L. *Ethics: Alternatives and Issues*. Grand Rapids: Zondervan, 1971.

Gula, Richard M. *Reason Informed by Faith: Foundations of Catholic Morality*. New York: Paulist, 1989.

Gustafson, James M. *Ethics from a Theocentric Perspective*. 2 vols. Chicago: University of Chicago Press, 1981.

——. *Protestant and Roman Catholic Ethics*. Chicago: University of Chicago Press, 1979.

*Hauerwas, Stanley. *A Community of Character: Toward a Constructive Social Ethics*. Notre Dame: University of Notre Dame Press, 1981.

——. *The Peaceable Kingdom: A Primer in Christian Ethics*. Notre Dame: University of Notre Dame Press, 1983.

Henry, Carl F.H. *Christian Personal Ethics*. Grand Rapids: Eerdmans, 1957.

*Holmes, Arthur F. *Ethics: Approaching Moral Decisions*. Downers Grove: InterVarsity, 1984.

*Long, Jr., Edward L. *A Survey of Christian Ethics*. New York: Oxford University Press, 1982.

Mahoney, John. *The Making of Moral Theology: A Study of the Roman Catholic Tradition*. Oxford: Clarendon, 1987.

Mott, Stephen C. *Biblical Ethics and Social Change*. New York: Oxford University Press, 1982.

*Niebuhr, H. Richard. *The Responsible Self: An Essay in Christian Moral Philosophy*. New York: Harper & Row, 1963.

*Niebuhr, Reinhold. *Moral Man and Immoral Society*. New York: Scribner's, 1948.

O'Connell, Timothy E. *Principles for a Catholic Morality*. New York: Seabury, 1978.

O'Donovan, Oliver. *Resurrection and Moral Order—An Outline for Evangelical Ethics*. Grand Rapids: Eerdmans, 1986.

*Ramsey, Paul. *Deeds and Rules in Christian Ethics*. New York: Scribner's, 1967.

Stott, John R.W. *Decisive Issues Facing Christians Today*. Grand Rapids: Fleming R. Revell, 1990.

Thielicke, Helmut. *Theological Ethics*. 3 vols. Philadelphia: Fortress, 1966-81.

White, Reginald E.O. *Christian Ethics: The Historical Development*. Atlanta: John Knox, 1981.

*Wilkens, Steve. *Beyond Bumper Sticker Ethics*. Downers Grove: InterVarsity, 1995.

Winter, Gibson, ed. *Social Ethics: Issues in Ethics and Society*. New York: Harper & Row, 1968.

Wogaman, J. Philip. *Christian Moral Judgement*. Louisville: Westminster/John Knox, 1989.

Philosophical Theology

Philosophical theology represents the study of theology where it intersects with important issues of philosophical debate, possibly drawing upon philosophy for religious insight.

(See also Apologetics, Reason)

*Abraham, William J. *An Introduction to the Philosophy of Religion*. Englewood Cliffs, NJ: Prentice-Hall, 1985.

*Allen, Diogenes. *Philosophy for Understanding Theology*. Louisville: Westminster/John Knox, 1986.

*Brown, Colin. *Christianity and Western Thought*. Vol 1. Downers Grove: InterVarsity, 1990.

——. *Philosophy and the Christian Faith*. Chicago: Inter-varsity, 1969.

*Evans, Stephen C., ed. *Contours of Christian Philosophy*. 7 vols. Downers Grove: InterVarsity, 1982-1991.

Flew, Antony, and Alasdair C. MacIntyre. *New Essays in Philosophical Theology*. New York: Macmillan, 1955.

Hick, John. *An Interpretation of Religion: Humanity's Responses to the Transcendent*. New Haven: Yale University Press, 1989.

Morris, Thomas V., ed. *Philosophy and the Christian Faith*. Notre Dame: University of Notre Dame Press, 1988.

*Pelikan, Jaroslav J. *The Melody of Theology: A Philosophical Dictionary*. Cambridge, MA: Harvard University Press, 1988.

Reese, William L. *Dictionary of Philosophy and Religion: Eastern and Western Thought*. Atlantic Highlands, NJ: Humanities, 1980.

Sauter, Gerhard. *The Question of Meaning: A Theological and Philosophical Orientation*. Grand Rapids: Eerdmans, 1995.

Vroom, H.M. *Religions and the Truth: Philosophical Reflections and Perspectives*. Grand Rapids: Eerdmans, 1989.

Wainwright, William J. *Philosophy of Religion: An Annotated Bibliography of Twentieth-Century Writings in English*. New York: Garland, 1978.

Practical Theology

Practical theology pertains to the practical applications of theology, particularly with regard to the Christian life and ministry.

(See also Church, Liturgy, Ministry, Sacraments, Worship)

*Anderson, Ray S. *Ministry on the Fireline: A Practical Theology for an Empowered Church*. Downers Grove: InterVarsity, 1993.

Arens, Edmund. *Christopraxis: A Theology of Action*. Minneapolis: Fortress, 1995.

*Atkinson, David J., and David F. Field, eds. *New Dictionary of Christian Ethics and Pastoral Theology*. Downers Grove: InterVarsity, 1995.

*Berkeley, James D., ed. *Leadership Handbooks of Practical Theology*. Grand Rapids: Baker, 1992.

Browning, Don S. *A Fundamental Practical Theology: Descriptive and Strategic Proposals*. Minneapolis: Augsburg Fortress, 1991.

Browning, Don S., ed. *Practical Theology*. San Francisco: Harper & Row, 1983.

Davies, John G., ed. *The New Westminster Dictionary of Liturgy and Worship*. Philadelphia: Westminster, 1986.

Forrester, Duncan B., ed. *Theology and Practice*. London: Epworth, 1990.

*Kinghorn, Kenneth C., ed. *A Celebration of Ministry*. Wilmore, KY: Francis Asbury, 1982.

O'Meara, Thomas F. *Theology of Ministry*. New York: Paulist, 1983.

Osborne, Grant R., ed. *An Annotated Bibliography on the Bible and the Church*. Deerfield, IL: Trinity Evangelical Divinity School, 1982.

*Pittman, Don A., et al., eds. *Ministry and Theology in Global Perspective: Contemporary Challenges for the Church*. Grand Rapids: Eerdmans, 1996.

*Poling, James N., and Donald E. Miller. *Foundations for a Practical Theology of Ministry*. Nashville: Abingdon, 1985.

Schillebeeckx, Edward. *The Church with a Human Face: A New and Expanded Theology of Ministry*. New York: Crossroad, 1985.

Stuhlmueller, Carol, ed. *The Collegeville Pastoral Dictionary of Biblical Theology*. Collegeville, MN: Liturgical, 1994.

Turnbull, Ralph G., ed. *Baker's Dictionary of Practical Theology*. Grand Rapids: Baker, 1967.

Systematic Theology

Systematic theology is sometimes considered the development of a coherent system of Christian belief. Others consider systematic theology to represent the methodical attempt to deal with the breadth of Christian belief. In this book, the latter (and broader) understanding of the term will be used to discuss the classic texts of Christian theology.

(See Notable Theologians, Doctrines)

NOTABLE THEOLOGIANS

The following writers represent notable Christian contributors to the development of Christian belief. They wrote at a variety of times and places in church history, but each had significant impact upon the development of theology. It is impossible, of course, to include everyone of note in church history. But these writers represent formative Christian thinkers, whose writings should be studied in the attempt to understand historic Christian beliefs.

One should read primary resources of theology from throughout the whole of church history. Although contemporary resources are important for the development of our theological understanding, such resources are built upon centuries of religious insight that is equally important. We should never be satisfied with reading secondary literature about formative theologians from the past. Reading, understanding and appreciating the writings of classic Christian authors should be considered essential to our theological reflections.

Few of the following authors represent systematic theologians in the sense that they attempted to create a system of Christian belief. But they did attempt to deal with a breadth of Christian beliefs.

Apostolic Period

Early Christian Writings. New York: Penguin Books, 1968.

The Faith of the Early Fathers. Collegeville, MN: Liturgical, 1970.

**Apostolic Fathers, Justin Martyr and Irenaeus*. Ante-Nicene Fathers, vol. 1. Ed. A.C. Coxe. Grand Rapids: Eerdmans, 1956.

Hermas, Tatian, Athenagoras, Theophilus, Clement of Alexandria. Ante-Nicene Fathers, vol. 2. Ed. A.C. Coxe. Grand Rapids: Eerdmans, 1956.

Ante-Nicene Period

*Origen. *On First Principles*. Gloucester, MA: Peter Smith, 1966.

Oulton, John E.L. *Alexandrian Christianity: Selected Translations of Clement and Origen*. The Library of Christian Classics. Philadelphia: Westminster, 1954.

**Tertullian*. The Ante-Nicene Fathers, vol. 3. Ed. A.C. Coxe. Grand Rapids: Eerdmans, 1956.

Hippolytus, Cyprian, Caius, Novation, Appendix. The Ante-Nicene Fathers, vol. 5. Ed. A.C. Coxe. Grand Rapids: Eerdmans, 1956.

Greenslade, Stanley L., ed. *Early Latin Theology: Selections from Tertullian, Cyprian, Ambrose, and Jerome*. The Library of Christian Classics. Eds. John Baillie, et al. London: SCM, 1956.

Patristic Period

*Ambrose. *Select Works and Letters*. Ed. H. de Romestin. A Select Library of Nicene and Post-Nicene Fathers, 2nd ed., vol. 10. Eds. Philip Schaff, et al. Grand Rapids: Eerdmans, 1956.

*Athanasius. *Select Works and Letters*. Ed. A. Robertson. A Select Library of Nicene and Post-Nicene Fathers, 2nd series, vol. 4. Eds. Philip Schaff, et al. Grand Rapids: Eerdmans, 1956.

Augustine. *Augustine: Earlier Writings*. Ed. John H.S. Burleigh. The Library of Christian Classics. Louisville: Westminster/John Knox, 1979.

——. *Augustine: Later Works*. Ed. John Burnaby. The Library of Christian Classics. Louisville: Westminster/John Knox, 1979.

*——. *St. Augustine*. Eds. A.H. Newman, et al. A Select Library of Nicene and Post-Nicene Fathers of the Christian Church. First series, vols. 1-6. Eds. Philip Schaff, et al. Grand Rapids: Eerdmans, 1956.

*Basil. *Letters and Select Works*. Ed. B. Jackson. A Select Library of Nicene and Post-Nicene Fathers, 2nd series, vol. 8. Eds. Philip Schaff, et al. Grand Rapids: Eerdmans, 1956.

Benedict. *Rule*. Westminster, MD: Christian Classics, 1972.

Boethius. *The Consolation of Philosophy*. New York: Penguin Books, 1976.

Cassian, John. *Works*. Ed. E.C.S. Gibson. A Select Library of Nicene and Post-Nicene Fathers, 2nd series, vol. 11. Eds. Philip Schaff, et al. Grand Rapids: Eerdmans, 1956.

Chrysostom, John. *In Praise of St. Paul*. Boston: Daughters of St. Paul, 1964.

*——. *On the Priesthood; Ascetic Treatises; Select Homilies and Letters; Homilies on the Statues*. A Select Library of Nicene and Post-Nicene Fathers, 2nd series, vol. 9. Eds. Philip Schaff, et al. Grand Rapids: Eerdmans, 1956.

Cyril of Jerusalem. *Orations and Letters*. Ed. C.G. Browne and J.E. Swallow. A Select Library of Nicene and Post-Nicene Fathers, 2nd series, vol. 7. Eds. Philip Schaff, et al. Grand Rapids: Eerdmans, 1956.

Dionysius the Areopagite. *Divine Names and Mystical Theology*. Naperville, IL: Alec R. Allenson, 1920.

Eusebius. *The History of the Church*. Minneapolis: Augsburg, 1975.

*Gregory of Nyssa. *Dogmatic Treatises*. Ed. V.W. Moore and H.A. Willson. A Select Library of Nicene and Post-Nicene Fathers, 2nd series, vol. 5. Eds. Philip Schaff, et al. Grand Rapids: Eerdmans, 1956.

Gregory the Great. *Works*. Ed. C.L. Feltoe. A Select Library of Nicene and Post-Nicene Fathers, 2nd series, vol. 12. Eds. Philip Schaff, et al. Grand Rapids: Eerdmans, 1956.

Hilary of Poitiers. *Select Works*. A Select Library of Nicene and Post-Nicene Fathers, 2nd series, vol. 9. Eds. Philip Schaff, et al. Grand Rapids: Eerdmans, 1956.

*Jerome. *Letters and Select Works*. Ed. W.H. Fremantle. A Select Library of Nicene and Post-Nicene Fathers, 2nd series, vol. 6. Eds. Philip Schaff, et al. Grand Rapids: Eerdmans, 1956.

John of Damascus. *Exposition of the Orthodox Faith*. A Select Library of Nicene and Post-Nicene Fathers, 2nd series, vol. 9. Eds. Philip Schaff, et al. Grand Rapids: Eerdmans, 1956.

Leo the Great. *Works*. Ed. C.L. Feltoe. A Select Library of Nicene and Post-Nicene Fathers, 2nd series, vol. 12. Eds. Philip Schaff, et al. Grand Rapids: Eerdmans, 1956.

Sayings of the Desert Fathers. Kalamazoo: Cistercian Publications, 1975.

The Seven Ecumenical Councils. Ed. H.R. Percival. A Select Library of Nicene and Post-Nicene Fathers, 2nd series, vol. 14. Eds. Philip Schaff, et al. Grand Rapids: Eerdmans, 1956.

Severus, Sulpitius. *Works*. Ed. Alexander Roberts. A Select Library of Nicene and Post-Nicene Fathers, 2nd series, vol. 11. Eds. Philip Schaff, et al. Grand Rapids: Eerdmans, 1956.

Vincent of Lerins. *Commonitory*. Ed. C.A. Heurtley. A Select Library of Nicene and Post-Nicene Fathers, 2nd series, vol. 11. Eds. Philip Schaff. Grand Rapids: Eerdmans, 1956.

Medieval Period

*Anselm. *Basic Writings*. La Salle, IL: Copen Court, 1966.

Bernard of Clairvaux. *Treatise on Loving God*. Kalamozoo: Cistercian, 1974.

Bonaventura. *The Mind's Road to God*. Indianapolis: Bobbs-Merrill, 1953.

Duns Scotus, Johannes. *God and Creatures*. Princeton: Princeton University Press, 1975.

Eckhart, Meister. *Breakthrough: Meister Eckhart's Creation Spirituality*. Garden City, NY: Doubleday, 1980.

Fairweather, Eugene, ed. *A Scholastic Miscellany: Anselm to Ockham*. The Library of Christian Classics. Eds. John Baillie, et al. London: SCM, 1956.

Francis of Assisi. *Writings*. Chicago: Franciscan Herald, 1964.

John of the Cross. *John of the Cross: Selected Writings*. The Classics of Western Spirituality. New York: Paulist, 1987.

Petry, Ray C., ed. *Late Medieval Mysticism*. The Library of Christian Classics. Louisville: Westminster/John Knox, 1980.

Thomas Aquinas. *Aquinas on Nature and Grace*. Ed. A.M. Fairweather. Library of Christian Classics. Louisville: Westminster/John Knox, 1978.

*——. *Basic Writings of Saint Thomas Aquinas*. Ed. Anton C. Pegis. New York: Random House, 1945.

——. *Summa Theologiae: A Concise Translation*. Westminster, MD: Christian Classics, 1989.

*Thomas à Kempis. *The Imitation of Christ*. Ed. Frederic W. Farrar. New York: E.P. Dutton, 1976.

Reformation and Counter-Reformation Period

Calvin, John. *Calvin: Commentaries*. Ed. Joseph Haroutunian. The Library of Christian Classics. Louisville: Westminster/John Knox, 1979.

*——. *Institutes of the Christian Religion*. Ed. John T. McNeill. The Library of Christian Classics. 2 vols. Eds. John Baillie, et al. Philadelphia: Westminster, 1960.

——. *Theological Treatises*. The Library of Christian Classics. Eds. John Baillie, et al. London: SCM, 1954.

Council of Trent, 1545-63, Canons and Decrees. St. Louis: B. Herder, 1955.

*Erasmus, Desiderius, and Martin Luther. *Discourse on Free Will*. New York: Frederick Ungar, 1960.

Ignatius de Loyola. *Spiritual Exercises*. New York: Doubleday, 1964.

*Luther, Martin. *Selected Writings of Martin Luther*. 4 vols. Ed. Theodore G. Tappert. Philadelphia: Fortress, 1967.

*——. *Three Treatises*. Philadelphia: Fortress, 1960.

——. *Works*. 55 vols. Ed. Jaroslav Pelikan. St. Louis: Concordia, 1955-1986.

Melanchthon, Philipp. *Melancthon on Christian Doctrine*. Ed. Clyde L. Mauschreck. New York: Oxford University Press, 1965.

*Simons, Meno. *Complete Writings*. Ed. J.C. Wenger. Scottsdale, PA: Herald, 1956.

Tappert, Theodore G., ed. *The Book of Concord*. Philadelphia: Fortress, 1959.

Teresa of Avila. *The Way of Perfection*. Ed. E.A. Peers. New York: Doubleday, 1973.

Williams, George H. and Angel Mergal, eds. *Spiritual and Anabaptist Writers*. The Library of Christian Classics. Eds. John Baillie, et al. London: SCM, 1957.

Zwingli, Ulrich. *Selected Writings*. Philadelphia: University of Pennsylvania Press, 1972.

Post-Reformation Period

*Arminius, James. *The Works of James Arminius*. 3 vols. 1875 rpt.; Grand Rapids: Baker, 1992.

Bunyan, John. *Pilgrim's Progress*. New York: Penguin, 1965.

*Edwards, Jonathan. *The Works of Jonathan Edwards*. 9 vols. New Haven: Yale University Press, 1957-1985.

*Fox, George. *Journal*. Rev. ed. Ed. John L. Nickalls. Cambridge: University Press, 1952.

Hodge, Charles. *Systematic Theology*. 3 vols. New York: Scribner, Armstrong, 1876.

*Hooker, Richard. *Of the Laws of Ecclesiastical Polity*. New York: E.P. Dutton, 1954.

——. *Tractates & Sermons*. Ed. Speed Hill. Cambridge, MA: Belknap, 1990.

*Kierkegaard, Søren. *A Kierkegaard Anthology*. Ed. Robert Bretall. Princeton: Princeton University Press, 1946.

*Knox, John. *Works of John Knox*. 6 vols. Ed. David Laing. 1864 rpt.; New York: AMS, 1966.

Law, William. *A Serious Call to a Devout and Holy Life*. New York: E.P. Dutton, 1972.

*Pascal, Blaise. *Pensees*. New York: E.P. Dutton, 1958.

Reformed Dogmatics: Johannes Wollebius, Gisbert Voetius and Francis Turretin. Ed. J. W. Beardslee. Grand Rapids: Baker, 1977.

Schleiermacher, Friedrich. *Brief Outline of the Study of Theology*. Atlanta: John Knox, 1966.

——. *The Christian Faith*. Ed. H.R. Mackintosh and J.S. Steward. New York: Harper & Row, 1963.

*——. *On Religion: Speeches to Its Cultured Despisers*. New York: Frederick Ungar, 1955.

*Simons, Meno. *The Complete Writings of Meno Simons: Circa 1496-1561*. Ed. John C. Wenger. Scottdale, PA: Herald, 1956.

*Spener, Philipp J. *Pia Desideria*. Philadelphia: Fortress, 1974.

Strong, Augustus H. *Systematic Theology*. Philadelphia: Judson, 1907.

*Wesley, John. *The Works of John Wesley*. 33 vols (proposed). Oxford and Bicentennial eds. Nashville: Abingdon, 1975-.

Wollebius, Johannes, et al. *Reformed Dogmatics*. Ed. J.W. Beardslee. Grand Rapids: Baker, 1977.

Contemporary Period (Multi-Volume Works)

(See also Doctrines, Contemporary Theological Issues)

*Barth, Karl. *Church Dogmatics*. 4 vols in 13. New York: Scribner's, 1936-1969.

*Bloesch, Donald G. *Christian Foundations*. 7 vols. Downers Grove: InterVarsity, 1992-.

*Bonhoeffer, Dietrich. *Dietrich Bonhoeffer Works*. 17 vols. Minneapolis: Augsburg Fortress, 1995-.

Brunner, Emil. *Dogmatics*. 3 vols. Philadelphia: Westminster, 1950-1962.

Chafer, Lewis S. *Systematic Theology*. 8 vols. Dallas: Dallas Seminary Press, 1947.

Erickson, Millard J. *Christian Theology*. 3 vols. Grand Rapids: Baker, 1983-1985.

Garrett, James L. *Systematic Theology*. Grand Rapids: Eerdmans, 1990-1995.

Henry, Carl F.H. *God, Revelation, and Authority*. 6 vols. Waco, TX: Word Books, 1976-1983.

Lewis, Gordon R., and Bruce A. Demarest. *Integrative Theology*. 3 vols. Grand Rapids: Zondervan, 1987-1994.

McClendon, Jr. James W. *Systematic Theology*. 2 vols. Nashville: Abingdon, 1986-.

*Oden, Thomas C. *Systematic Theology*. 3 vols. San Francisco: Harper & Row, 1987-1992.

*Pannenberg, Wolfhart. *Systematic Theology*. 2 vols. Grand Rapids: Eerdmans, 1991-1994.

*Rahner, Karl. *Theological Investigations*. Vols 1-17, 20. Baltimore: Helicon, 1961-1981.

Thielicke, Helmut. *The Evangelical Faith*. 3 vols. Grand Rapids: Eerdmans, 1974-1982.

Tillich, Paul. *Systematic Theology*. 3 vols. Chicago: University of Chicago Press, 1951-1963.

Weber, Otto. *Foundations of Dogmatics*. 2 vols. Grand Rapids: Eerdmans, 1981-1983.

Williams, J. Rodman. *Renewal Theology*. 3 vols. Grand Rapids: Zondervan, 1988-1992.

Multi-Volume Critical Editions of Classical Christian Texts

*Baillie, John, et al, eds. *The Library of Christian Classics*. 26 vols. London: SCM, 1953-1969.

Deferrari, Roy J., ed. *The Fathers of the Church*. 66 vols. Gaithersburg, MD: Consortium Books, 1948-

*Dillenberger, John, ed. *A Library of Protestant Thought*. 13 vols. New York: Oxford University Press, 1964-1972.

Page, T.E., et al, eds. *The Loeb Classical Library*. Cambridge, MA: Harvard University Press, 1913-

*Payne, Richard J., ed. *Classics of Western Spirituality*. New York: Paulist, 1978-

Roberts, Alexander, and James Donaldson, eds. *The Ante-Nicene Fathers: Translations of the Writings of the Fathers Down to A.D. 325*. 10 vols. Rev. by A. Cleveland Coxe. Grand Rapids: Eerdmans, 1950-1951.

*Schaff, Philip, ed. *A Select Library of Nicene and Post-Nicene Fathers of the Christian Church.* First Series, 14 vols. Eds. Philip Schaff, et al. New York: Christian Literature Company, 1886-1900. Second Series, 14 vols. Grand Rapids: Eerdmans, 1952-1957.

Quasten, Johannes, and J. Plump, eds. *Ancient Christian Writers.* New York: Paulist, 1946-

DOCTRINES

The following doctrines represent historic themes of Christian belief. It is not an exhaustive list, but it provides an overview of Christian beliefs of import throughout church history.

Most of the writings of historic theologians listed in the previous section are not duplicated below. However, in many instances, the following doctrines are discussed in the work of those classic Christian writers, whose writings are extensive as well as comprehensive. So the works of historic theologians should also be read when investigating a specific doctrine.

Additional areas of Christian belief are dealt with later in the section on Contemporary Theological Issues. There theological issues more reflective of modern concerns are covered.

Angels

Caird, George B. *Principalities and Powers*. Oxford: Clarendon, 1956.

*Carr, Wesley. *Angels and Principalities*. New York: Cambridge University Press, 1981.

*Garrett, Duane A. *Angels and the New Spirituality*. Nashville: Broadman & Holman, 1995.

Gilmore, G. Don. *Angels, Angels, Everywhere*. New York: Pilgrim, 1981.

Graham, Billy. *Angels*. Garden City, NY: Doubleday, 1975.

Lewis, James R., and Evelyn D. Oliver. *Angels, A to Z*. Ed. Kelle S. Sisung. Detroit: Visible Ink, 1996.

Apologetics

Brown, Colin. *Philosophy and the Christian Faith*. London: InterVarsity Fellowship, 1973.

Bruce, F.F. *The Apostolic Defense of the Gospel*. London: InterVarsity Fellowship, 1959.

Carnell, Edward J. *An Introduction to Christian Apologetics*. Grand Rapids: Eerdmans, 1952.

Corduan, Winfried. *Reasonable Faith: Basic Christian Apologetics*. Nashville: Broadman & Holman, 1994.

Dulles, Avery. *A History of Apologetics*. New York: Corpus, 1971.

Geisler, Norman L., and Ron Brooks. *When Skeptics Ask: A Handbook of Christian Evidences*. Wheaton, IL: Victor, 1990.

*Gill, Jerry H. *Faith in Dialogue: A Christian Apologetic*. Waco, TX: Jarrell, 1985.

*Lewis, C. S. *Mere Christianity*. New York: Macmillan, 1960.

Lewis, Gordon R. *Testing Christianity's Truth Claims: Approaches to Christian Apologetics*. Chicago: Moody, 1976.

*Mitchell, Basil S. *The Justification of Religious Belief*. New York: Macmillan, 1973.

*Phillips, Timothy R., and Dennis L. Okholm, eds. *Christian Apologetics in the Postmodern World*. Downers Grove: InterVarsity, 1995.

Ramm, Bernard L. *Varieties of Christian Apologetics*. Grand Rapids: Baker, 1961.

Reid, John K.S. *Christian Apologetics*. Grand Rapids: Eerdmans, 1970.

Richardson, Alan. *Christian Apologetics*. New York: Harper & Row, 1947.

Sproul, R.C., et al. *Classical Apologetics: A Rational Defense of the Christian Faith and a Critique of Presuppositional Apologetic*. Grand Rapids: Zondervan, 1984.

*Swinburne, Richard. *The Coherence of Theism*. Oxford: Clarendon, 1977.

*Taylor, Daniel. *The Myth of Certainty: Asking Questions in Pursuit of Meaning*. Grand Rapids: Zondervan, 1992.

Theissen, Gerd. *A Critical Faith: A Case for Religion*. Philadelphia: Fortress, 1979.

Trueblood, D. Elton. *A Place to Stand*. New York: Harper & Row, 1969.

Van Til, Cornelius. *The Defense of the Faith*. Philadelphia: Presbyterian and Reformed Publishing, 1955.

Wolfe, David L. *Epistemology, The Justification of Belief*. Downers Grove: InterVarsity, 1982.

Assurance

(See also Salvation)

Anderson, David. *Conditional Security*. 1946 rpt.; Salem, OH: Schmul, 1985.

*Marshall, I. Howard. *Kept by the Power of God*. London: Epworth, 1969.

McClendon, Jr., James W., and James Smith. *Understanding Religious Convictions*. Notre Dame: University of Notre Dame Press, 1975.

Newbigin, Lesslie. *Proper Confidence: Faith, Doubt, and Certainty in Christian Discipleship*. Grand Rapids: Eerdmans, 1995.

Plantinga, Jr., Cornelius. *Assurances of the Heart*. Grand Rapids: Zondervan, 1993.

*Purkiser, W.T. *Security*. Kansas City: Beacon Hill, 1956.

Atonement

(See also Salvation)

Aulén, Gustav. *Christus Victor*. New York: Macmillan, 1931.

*Baillie, Donald M. *God Was in Christ*. New York: Scribner's 1948.

Brunner, Emil. *The Mediator*. London: Lutterworth, 1952.

Campbell, John McLeod. *The Nature of the Atonement*. London: J. Clarke, 1959.

Culpepper, Robert H. *Interpreting the Atonement*. Grand Rapids: Eerdmans, 1966.

Denney, James. *The Christian Doctrine of Reconciliation*. New York: Doran, 1917.

——. *The Death of Christ*. London: Tyndale, 1951.

Dillistone, Frederick W. *The Christian Understanding of Atonement*. Digswell Place, England: J. Nisbet, 1968.

Fiddes, Paul S. *Past Event and Present Salvation: The Christian Idea of Atonement*. Louisville: Westminster/John Knox, 1989.

Forsyth, Peter T. *The Cruciality of the Cross*. London: Hodder and Stoughton, 1910.

——. *The Work of Christ*. London: Hodder and Stoughton, 1910.

Franks, Robert S. *The Work of Christ: A Historical Study of Christian Doctrine*. London: Thomas Nelson, 1962.

Gunton, Colin E. *The Actuality of Atonement: A Study of Metaphor, Rationality, and the Christian Tradition*. Grand Rapids: Eerdmans, 1989.

Hengel, Martin. *The Atonement: The Origins of the Doctrine in the New Testament*. Philadelphia: Fortress, 1981.

Hodge, Alexander A. *The Atonement*. Grand Rapids: Eerdmans, 1953.

Hodgson, Leonard. *The Doctrine of the Atonement*. London: Nisbet, 1951.

Mackintosh, H.R. *The Christian Experience of Forgiveness*. London: Collins, 1954.

*Martin, Ralph P. *Reconciliation: A Study of Paul's Theology*. Atlanta: John Knox, 1981.

*McGrath, Alister E. *What Was God Doing on the Cross*? Grand Rapids: Zondervan, 1993.

*Moltmann, Jürgen. *The Crucified God*. London: SCM, 1974.

*Morris, Leon. *The Apostolic Preaching of the Cross*. Grand Rapids: Eerdmans, 1976.

Owen, John. *The Death of Death in the Death of Christ*. London: Banner of Truth, 1959.

Schillebeeckx, Edward. *Christ: The Experience of Jesus as Lord*. Trans. John Bowden. New York: Seabury, 1980.

Stott, John R.W. *The Cross of Christ*. Downers Grove: InterVarsity, 1986.

Taylor, Vincent. *The Atonement in New Testament Teaching*. London: Epworth, 1940.

——. *Forgiveness and Reconciliation*. London: Macmillan, 1948.

Wallace, Ronald, S. *The Atoning Death of Christ*. Westchester, IL: Crossway Books, 1981.

Young, Frances M. *Sacrifice and the Death of Christ*. London: SPCK, 1975.

Authority

(See also Bible-Biblical Authority)

Forsyth, Peter T. *The Principle of Authority*. London: Hodder and Stoughton, 1952.

Geldenhuys, Johannes N. *Supreme Authority*. Edinburgh: Marshall, Morgan & Scott, 1953.

Henry, Carl. F.H. *God, Revelation, and Authority*. 6 vols. Waco, TX.: Word Books, 1979-1983.

*Johnson, Robert C. *Authority in Protestant Theology*. Philadelphia: Westminster, 1959.

Lash, Nicholas. *Voices of Authority*. London: Sheed and Ward, 1976.

Lloyd-Jones, D. Martyn. *Authority*. Chicago: InterVarsity, 1958.

*Packer, James I. *Freedom, Authority and Scripture*. Leicester: InterVarsity, 1981.

*Ramm, Bernard L. *The Pattern of Religious Authority*. Grand Rapids: Eerdmans, 1959.

Russell, Letty M. *Household of Freedom: Authority in Feminist Theology*. Louisville: Westminster/John Knox, 1987.

Williams, R. Ralph. *Authority in the Apostolic Age*. London: SCM, 1950.

Baptism

(See also Baptism-Infant Baptism, Sacraments)

Barth, Karl. *The Teaching of the Church Regarding Baptism*. London: SCM, 1948.

Carson, Alexander. *Baptism: Its Modes and Subjects*. Grand Rapids: Kregel Publications, 1981.

*Cullmann, Oscar. *Baptism in the New Testament*. London: SCM, 1964.

Fisher, John D.C. *Christian Initiation: Baptism in the Medieval West*. London: SPCK, 1965.

——. *Christian Initiation: The Reformation Period*. London: SPCK, 1970.

Kavanagh, Aidan. *The Shape of Baptism: The Rite of Christian Initiation.* New York: Pueblo, 1978.

Lampe, Geoffrey W.H. *The Seal of the Spirit: A Study in the Doctrine of Baptism and Confirmation in the New Testament and the Fathers.* New York: Longmans/Green, 1967.

*Marty, Martin E. *Baptism.* Philadelphia: Muhlenberg, 1962.

Mitchell, Leonal L. *Baptismal Anointing.* London: SPCK, 1966.

Osborne, Kenan B. *The Christian Sacraments of Initiation.* New York: Paulist, 1987.

Schnackenburg, Rudolf. *Baptism in the Thought of St. Paul.* New York: Herder and Herder, 1964.

Searle, Mark. *Christening: The Making of Christians.* Collegeville, MN: Liturgical, 1980.

Wainwright, Geoffrey. *Christian Initiation.* London: Lutterworth, 1969.

Walsh, Liam G. *The Sacraments of Initiation: Baptism, Confirmation, Eucharist.* London: Chapman, 1988.

Warns, Johannes. *Baptism.* London: Paternoster, 1957.

Whitaker, Edward C. *Documents of the Baptismal Liturgy.* London: SPCK, 1960.

Baptism: Infant Baptism

(See also Baptism)

Aland, Kurt. *Did the Early Church Baptize Infants?* Philadelphia: Westminster, 1963.

*Bromiley, Geoffrey W. *The Baptism of Infants.* London: Church Book Room, 1955.

*Jeremias, Joachim. *Infant Baptism in the First Four Centuries*. London: SCM, 1960.

*Jewett, Paul K. *Infant Baptism and the Covenant of Grace*. Grand Rapids: Eerdmans, 1978.

Marcel, Pierre C. *The Biblical Doctrine of Infant Baptism*. London: James Clarke, 1953.

Bible

*Barr, James. *The Bible in the Modern World*. New York: Harper & Row, 1973.

*Barth, Karl. *The Word of God and the Word of Man*. Grand Rapids: Zondervan, 1935.

Berkouwer, G.C. *Holy Scripture*. Ed. Jack B. Rogers. Grand Rapids: Eerdmans, 1975.

*Bruce, F.F. *The Books and the Parchments*. London: Pickering & Inglis, 1950.

Brueggemann, Walter. *The Creative Word*. Philadelphia: Fortress, 1982.

*Hatch, Nathan O., and Mark A. Noll. *The Bible in America*. New York: Oxford University Press, 1982.

Kelsey, David H. *The Uses of Scripture in Recent Theology*. Philadelphia: Fortress, 1979.

Marxsen, Willi. *The New Testament as the Church's Book*. Philadelphia: Fortress, 1972.

McDonald, Hugh D. *What the Bible Teaches About the Bible*. Wheaton, IL: Tyndale, 1979.

*McKim, Donald K. *What Christians Believe About the Bible*. Nashville: Thomas Nelson, 1985.

Nineham, Dennis E. *The Use and Abuse of the Bible: A Study of the Bible in an Age of Rapid Cultural Change*. New York: Barnes & Noble Books, 1976.

*Pinnock, Clark H. *The Scripture Principle*. San Francisco: Harper & Row, 1984.

Richardson, Alan. *The Bible in the Age of Science*. London: SCM, 1961.

Bible: Canon

*Barr, James. *Holy Scripture: Canon, Authority and Criticism*. Philadelphia: Westminster, 1983.

Beckwith, Roger T. *The Old Testament Canon of the New Testament Church and Its Background in Early Judaism*. Grand Rapids: Eerdmans, 1985.

Blenkinsopp, Joseph. *Prophecy and Canon*. Notre Dame: University of Notre Dame Press, 1977.

Campenhausen, Hans von. *The Formation of the Christian Bible*. London: A. and C. Black, 1972.

*Carson, Donald A., and John D. Woodbridge, eds. *Hermeneutics, Authority and Canon*. Grand Rapids: Academie Books, 1986.

*Childs, Brevard S. *The New Testament as Canon: An Introduction*. Philadelphia: Fortress, 1984.

Farmer, William R. *Jesus and the Gospel: Tradition, Scripture and Canon*. Philadelphia: Fortress, 1982.

Filson, Floyd V. *Which Books Belong to the Bible?* Philadelphia: Westminster, 1957.

Goodspeed, Edgar J. *The Formation of the New Testament*. Chicago: University of Chicago Press, 1926.

Grant, Robert M. *The Formation of the New Testament*. New York: Harper & Row, 1965.

Harris, R. Laird. *The Inspiration and Canonicity of the Bible*. Grand Rapids: Zondervan, 1971.

McDonald, Lee M. *The Formation of the Christian Biblical Canon*. Nashville: Abingdon, 1988.

*Metzger, Bruce M. *The Canon of the New Testament: Its Origin, Development, and Significance*. New York: Oxford University Press, 1987.

Sanders, James A. *Torah and Canon*. Philadelphia: Fortress, 1972.

Bible: Biblical Interpretation (Hermeneutics)

Armerding, Carl E. *The Old Testament and Criticism*. Grand Rapids: Eerdmans, 1983.

Barbour, Robert S. *Traditio-Historical Criticism of the Gospels*. London: SPCK, 1972.

*Barr, James. *Holy Scripture: Canon, Authority and Criticism*. Philadelphia: Westminster, 1983.

*——. *Old and New in Interpretation*. New York: Harper & Row, 1966.

Barthes, Roland, et al. *Structural Analysis and Biblical Exegesis: Interpretational Essays*. Pittsburgh: Pickwick, 1974.

Blackman, Edwin C. *Biblical Interpretation*. Philadelphia: Westminster, 1957.

Bleicher, Josef. *Contemporary Hermeneutics*. London: Routledge & K. Paul, 1980.

Braaten, Carl E. *History and Hermeneutics*. Philadelphia: Westminster, 1966.

*Braaten, Carl E., and Robert W. Jenson, eds. *Reclaiming the Bible for the Church*. Grand Rapids: Eerdmans, 1995.

Brown, Raymond E. *The Critical Meaning of the Bible*. New York: Paulist, 1981.

Carson, Donald A., ed. *Biblical Interpretation and the Church*. Nashville: Thomas Nelson, 1984.

*Carson, Donald A., and John D. Woodbridge, eds. *Hermeneutics, Authority and Canon*. Grand Rapids: Academie Books, 1986.

*Childs, Brevard S. *Introduction to the Old Testament as Scripture*. Philadelphia: Fortress, 1979.

Epp, Eldon J., and George W. MacRae, eds. *The New Testament and Its Modern Interpreters*. Philadelphia: Fortress, 1987.

Farrar, Frederic W. *History of Interpretation*. Grand Rapids: Baker, 1961.

Funk, Robert W. *Language, Hermeneutics and Word of God*. New York: Harper & Row, 1966.

Goppelt, Leonhard. *Typos: The Typological Interpretation of the Old Testament in the New*. Grand Rapids: Eerdmans, 1982.

Grant, Robert M., and David Tracy. *A Short History of the Interpretation of the Bible*. Philadelphia: Fortress, 1984.

Hayes, John H., and Carl R. Holladay. *Biblical Exegesis: A Beginner's Handbook*. Atlanta: John Knox, 1987.

Knight, Douglas A., and Gene M. Tucker, eds. *The Hebrew Bible and Its Modern Interpreters*. Philadelphia: Fortress, 1985.

Krentz, Edgar. *The Historical-Critical Method*. Philadelphia: Fortress, 1975.

Kümmel, Werner G. *The New Testament: The History of the Investigation of its Problems*. Nashville: Abingdon, 1972.

*Küng, Hans, and Jürgen Moltmann. *Conflicting Ways of Interpreting the Bible*. New York: Seabury, 1980.

*Ladd, George E. *The New Testament and Criticism*. Grand Rapids: Eerdmans, 1967.

*Marshall, I. Howard., ed. *New Testament Interpretation*. Grand Rapids: Eerdmans, 1977.

McKnight, Edgar V. *Meaning in Texts*. Philadelphia: Fortress, 1978.

*Metzger, Bruce M. *The Text of the New Testament*. New York: Oxford University Press, 1968.

Mueller-Vollmer, Kurt, ed. *The Hermeneutics Reader*. New York: Continuum, 1985.

Nineham, Dennis E., ed. *The Church's Use of the Bible Past and Present*. London: SPCK, 1963.

Osborne, Grant R. *The Hermeneutical Spiral*. Downers Grove: InterVarsity, 1991.

Patte, Daniel. *Structural Exegesis for New Testament Critics*. Philadelphia: Fortress, 1978.

Perrin, Norman. *What is Redaction Criticism*? Philadelphia: Fortress, 1969.

Polzin, Robert M. *Biblical Structuralism: Method and Subjectivity in the Study of Ancient Texts*. Philadelphia: Fortress, 1977.

Redlich, Edwin B. *Form Criticism*. New York: Scribner's, 1939.

Ricoeur, Paul. *Interpretation Theory*. Fort Worth: Texas Christian University Press, 1976.

——. *Hermeneutics and the Human Sciences*. New York: Cambridge University Press, 1981.

Robinson, James M., and John B. Cobb, Jr. *The New Hermeneutic*. Vol. 2. New York: Harper & Row, 1964.

*Rogers, Jack B., and Donald K. McKim. *The Authority and Interpretation of the Bible. An Historical Approach.* San Francisco: Harper & Row, 1979.

*Sanders, James A. *Canon and Community: A Guide to Canonical Criticism.* Philadelphia: Fortress, 1984.

Smart, James D. *The Interpretation of Scripture.* Philadelphia: Westminster, 1961.

Stuhlmacher, Peter. *Historical Criticism and Theological Interpretation of Scripture.* Philadelphia: Fortress, 1977.

Thiselton, Anthony C. *The Two Horizons: New Testament Hermeneutics and Philosophical Description.* Grand Rapids: Eerdmans, 1980.

Tracy, David. *Plurality and Ambiguity: Hermeneutics, Religion, Hope.* San Francisco: Harper & Row, 1987.

Walhout, Clarence, et al. *The Responsibility of Hermeneutics.* Grand Rapids: Eerdmans, 1985.

Wood, James D. *The Interpretation of the Bible.* London: Duckworth, 1958.

Bible: Inspiration

Achtemeier, Paul J. *The Inspiration of Scripture.* Philadelphia: Westminster, 1980.

Harris, R. Laird. *The Inspiration and Canonicity of the Bible.* Grand Rapids: Zondervan, 1971.

*Marshall, I. Howard. *Biblical Inspiration.* Grand Rapids: Eerdmans, 1983.

*Orr, James. *Revelation and Inspiration.* Grand Rapids: Eerdmans, 1952.

*Packer, James I. *God Has Spoken.* Downers Grove: InterVarsity, 1979.

*Pinnock, Clark H. *Biblical Revelation, The Foundation of Christian Theology*. Phillipsburg, NJ: Presbyterian and Reformed Publishing, 1985.

Vawter, Bruce. *Biblical Inspiration*. Philadelphia: Westminster, 1972.

Warfield, B.B. *The Inspiration and Authority of the Bible*. Philadelphia: Presbyterian and Reformed Publishing, 1970.

Bible: Biblical Truth/Trustworthiness

*Beegle, Dewey M. *Scripture, Tradition and Infallibility*. Grand Rapids: Eerdmans, 1973.

*Carson, Donald A., and John D. Woodbridge, eds. *Scripture and Truth*. Grand Rapids: Zondervan, 1983.

*Davis, Stephen T. *The Debate About the Bible*. Philadelphia: Westminster, 1977.

Geisler, Norman L. ed. *Inerrancy*. Grand Rapids: Zondervan, 1980.

Küng, Hans. *Infallible? An Inquiry*. Garden City, NY: Doubleday, 1971.

Loretz, Oswald. *The Truth of the Bible*. New York: Herder and Herder, 1968.

Montgomery, John W., ed. *God's Inerrant Word: An International Symposium on the Trustworthiness of Scripture*. Minneapolis: Bethany Fellowship, 1974.

Moody, Dale. *The Word of Truth*. Grand Rapids: Eerdmans, 1981.

Young, Edward J. *Thy Word is Truth*. Grand Rapids: Eerdmans, 1957.

Bible: Biblical Authority

Abba, Raymond. *The Nature and Authority of the Bible*. Philadelphia: Muhlenberg, 1959.

*Barr, James. *Holy Scripture: Canon, Authority and Criticism.* Philadelphia: Westminster, 1983.

*Carson, Donald A., and John D. Woodbridge, eds. *Hermeneutics, Authority and Canon*. Grand Rapids: Academie Books, 1986.

Cunliffe-Jones, Hubert. *The Authority of the Biblical Revelation*. Boston: Pilgrim, 1948.

Davies, Rupert. E. *The Problem of Authority in the Continental Reformers*. London: Epworth, 1946.

Dodd, C.H. *The Authority of the Bible*. New York: Harper & Row, 1958.

Packer, James I. *Freedom, Authority and Scripture*. Leicester: InterVarsity, 1981.

Reventlow, Henning G. *The Authority of the Bible and the Rise of the Modern World*. Trans. John Bowden. Philadelphia: Fortress, 1984.

Richardson, Alan, and Wolfgang Schweitzer, eds. *Biblical Authority*. London: SCM, 1951.

*Rogers, Jack B., and Donald K. McKim. *The Authority and Interpretation of the Bible, An Historical Approach*. San Francisco: Harper & Row, 1979.

Warfield, B.B. *The Inspiration and Authority of the Bible*. Philadelphia: Presbyterian and Reformed Publishing, 1970.

Christian Life

(See also Discipleship)

*Bonhoeffer, Dietrich. *Cost of Discipleship*. New York: Macmillan, 1951.

Collins, Kenneth J. *Soul Care: Deliverance and Renewal through the Christian Life*. Wheaton: BridgePoint, 1995.

*Foster, Richard J. *Celebration of Discipline.* San Francisco: Harper & Row, 1988.

Grenz, Stanley J. *Created for Community: Connecting Christian Belief with Christian Living.* Wheaton, IL: BridgePoint, 1996.

Hanks, Jr., Billie, and William A. Shell. *Discipleship.* Grand Rapids: Zondervan, 1993.

*Hauerwas, Stanley. *Character and the Christian Life.* San Antonio: Trinity University, 1975.

——. *A Community of Character.* Notre Dame: University of Notre Dame Press, 1981.

Jeanrond, Werner G. *Call and Response: The Challenge of Christian Life.* New York: Continuum, 1995.

Küng, Hans. *On Being a Christian.* Garden City, NY: Doubleday, 1976.

*LaCugna, Catherine M. *God for Us: The Trinity and Christian Life.* New York: HarperCollins, 1991.

Long, Grace D.C. *Passion and Reason: Womenviews of Christian Life.* Louisville: Westminster/John Knox, 1993.

Church (Ecclesiology)

*Barrett, C.K. *Church, Ministry and Sacraments in the New Testament.* Grand Rapids: Eerdmans, 1985.

Berkouwer, G.C. *The Church.* Grand Rapids: Eerdmans, 1976.

Bettenson, Henry, ed. *Documents of the Christian Church.* New York: Oxford University Press, 1970.

Brunner, Emil. *The Christian Doctrine of the Church, Faith, and Consummation.* Philadelphia: Westminster, 1962.

Cerfaux, Lucien *The Church in the Theology of St. Paul.* New York: Herder, 1959.

Clowney, Edmund P. *The Church*. Downers Grove: InterVarsity, 1995.

Cwiekowski, Frederick J. *The Beginnings of the Church*. New York: Paulist, 1988.

Dulles, Avery. *A Church to Believe In: Discipleship and the Dynamics of Freedom*. New York: Crossroad, 1982.

*——. *Models of the Church*. Rev. ed. New York: Doubleday, 1987.

Flew, R. Newton, ed. *The Nature of the Church*. London: SCM, 1952.

*Giles, Kevin. *What on Earth Is the Church*? Downers Grove: InterVarsity, 1995.

*Hodge, Charles. *Discussions in Church Polity*. New York: Charles Scribner's, 1878.

Kuiper, R.B. *The Glorious Body of Christ*. Grand Rapids: Eerdmans, 1958.

Küng, Hans. *The Church*. Garden City, NY.: Image Books, 1976.

Metz, Johannes B. *The Emergent Church*. New York: Crossroad, 1981.

Minear, Paul S. *Images of the Church in the New Testament*. London: Lutterworth, 1961.

*Moltmann, Jürgen. *The Church in the Power of the Spirit*. Minneapolis: Fortress, 1993.

Newbigin, Lesslie. *The Household of God: Lectures on the Nature of the Church*. New York: Friendship, 1954.

Smith, David L. *All God's People: A Theology of the Church*. Wheaton, IL: BridgePoint, 1996.

*Snyder, Howard A. *The Community of the King*. Downers Grove: InterVarsity, 1977.

*Stibbs, Alan. *God's Church: A Study in the Biblical Doctrine of the People of God*. Chicago: InterVarsity, 1959.

Conversion

(See also Faith, Repentance, Regeneration, Salvation)

Barry, William A. *Now Choose Life: Conversion as the Way to Life*. New York: Paulist, 1990.

Citron, Bernhard. *New Birth: A Study of the Evangelical Doctrine of Conversion in the Protestant Fathers*. Edinburgh: University Press, 1951.

Ervin, Howard M. *Conversion-Initiation and the Baptism in the Holy Spirit*. Peabody, MA: Hendrickson, 1985.

Gillespie, V. Bailey. *The Dynamics of Religious Conversion*. Birmingham: Religious Education Press, 1991.

Happel, Stephen, and James J. Walter. *Conversion and Discipleship: A Christian Foundation for Ethics and Doctrine*. Philadelphia: Fortress, 1986.

*Johnson, Cedric B., and H. Newton Malony. *Christian Conversion: Biblical and Psychological Perspectives*. Grand Rapids: Zondervan, 1981.

*Malony, H. Newton, and Samuel Southard, eds. *Handbook of Religious Conversion*. Birmingham: Religious Education, 1992.

Morrison, Karl F. *Understanding Conversion*. Charlottesville: University Press of Virginia, 1992.

Rambo, Lewis R. *Understanding Religious Conversion*. New Haven: Yale University Press, 1993.

Wallis, Jim. *The Call to Conversion*. New York: Harper & Row, 1981.

Creation

*Blocher, Henri. *In the Beginning*. Downers Grove: InterVarsity, 1984.

Burke, Derek. *Creation and Evolution*. Leicester: InterVarsity, 1985.

Clark, Robert E.D. *The Universe: Plan or Accident?* Philadelphia: Muhlenberg, 1962.

Cromartie, Michael, ed. *Creation at Risk? Religion, Science, and Environmentalism*. Grand Rapids: Eerdmans, 1995.

Frye, Roland Mushat, ed. *Is God a Creationist? The Religious Case Against Creation-Science*. New York: Scribner's, 1983.

Gilkey, Langdon. *Creationism on Trial*. Minneapolis: Winston, 1985.

——. *Maker of Heaven and Earth: A Study of the Christian Doctrine of Creation*. Garden City, NY: Doubleday, 1959.

*Hayes, Zachary. *What Are They Saying About Creation?* New York: Paulist, 1980.

Heim, Karl. *The World: Its Creation and Consummation*. Edinburgh: Oliver and Boyd, 1962.

Jaki, Stanley, L. *Cosmos and Creator, Science and Creation*. Edinburgh: Scottish Academic, 1980.

Moltmann, Jürgen. *God in Creation*. San Francisco: Harper & Row, 1985.

Moreland, J.P., ed. *The Creation Hypothesis*. Downers Grove: InterVarsity, 1994.

Morris, Henry, et. al. *Creation: Acts, Facts, Impacts*. San Diego: ICR Publishing, 1974.

Peacocke, Arthur R. *Creation and the World of Science*. New York: Oxford University Press, 1979.

*Ratzsch, Del. *The Battle of Beginnings: Why Neither Side Is Winning the Creation-Evolution Debate*. Downers Grove: InterVarsity, 1996.

*Van Till, Howard J., et al. *Portraits of Creation: Biblical and Scientific Perspectives on the World's Formation*. Grand Rapids: Eerdmans, 1990.

*——. *Science Held Hostage: What's Wrong with Creation-Science and Evolutionism*. Downers Grove: InterVarsity, 1988.

Worthing, Mark W. *God, Creation, and Contemporary Physics*. Minneapolis: Augsburg Fortress, 1995.

Creeds and Confessions

*Campbell, Ted A. *Christian Confessions: A Historical Introduction*. Louisville: Westminster/John Knox, 1996.

*Kelly, John N.D. *Early Christian Creeds*. 3rd ed. London: Longman, 1981.

*Leith, John H., ed. *Creeds of the Churches*, 3rd ed. Atlanta: John Knox, 1982.

Melton, J. Gordon, ed. *American Religious Creeds*. 3 vols. Liguori, MO: Liguori Publications, 1992.

Phillips, Timothy R., and Dennis L. Okholm, eds. *The Nature of Confession: Evangelicals and Postliberals in Conversation*. Downers Grove: InterVarsity, 1996.

Quick, Oliver C. *Doctrines of the Creed*. London: Nisbet and Co., 1947.

*Richardson, Alan. *Creeds in the Making: A Short Introduction to the History of Christian Doctrine*. Rev. ed. Valley Forge, PA: Trinity Press International, 1990.

*Schaff, Philip, ed. *The Creeds of the Christendom*. 3 vols. New York: Harper, 1877.

Young, Frances M. *The Making of the Creeds*. Valley Forge, PA: Trinity Press International, 1991.

Death

Aldwinckle, Russell. *Death in the Secular City*. Grand Rapids: Eerdmans, 1974.

Bailey, Lloyd R. *Biblical Perspectives on Death*. Philadelphia: Fortress, 1979.

*Connelly, Douglas. *After Life: What the Bible Really Says*. Downers Grove: InterVarsity, 1995.

Hick, John. *Death and Eternal Life*. New York: Harper & Row, 1976.

Martin-Achard, Robert. *From Death to Life*. Edinburgh: Oliver and Boyd, 1960.

McManners, John. *Death and the Enlightenment*. New York: Oxford University Press, 1981.

*Mills, Liston O., ed. *Perspectives on Death*. Nashville: Abingdon, 1969.

*Morris, Leon. *The Wages of Sin: An Examination of the New Testament Teaching on Death*. London: Tyndale, 1954.

Owen, John. *The Death of Death in the Death of Christ*. London: The Banner of Truth Trust, 1959.

Pelikan, Jaroslav J. *The Shape of Death: Life, Death, and Immortality in the Early Fathers*. New York: Abingdon, 1961.

Rahner, Karl. *On the Theology of Death*. New York: Herder and Herder, 1961.

Devil/Demons

Bainbridge, William S. *Satan's Power: A Deviant Psychotherapy Cult*. Berkeley: University of California Press, 1978.

*Barnhouse, Donald G. *The Invisible War*. Grand Rapids: Zondervan, 1965.

Kelly, Henry A. *The Devil, Demonology, and Witchcraft*. Garden City, NY: Doubleday, 1974.

*Lewis, Edwin. *The Creator and the Adversary*. New York: Abingdon-Cokesbury, 1948.

Montgomery, John W. *Principalities and Powers: The World of the Occult*. Minneapolis: Bethany Fellowship, 1973.

Pentecost, J. Dwight. *Your Adversary, the Devil*. Grand Rapids: Zondervan, 1969.

Russell, Jeffrey B. *Satan: The Early Christian Tradition*. Ithaca, NY: Cornell University Press, 1981.

Schlier, Heinrich. *Principalities and Powers in the New Testament*. Edinburgh: Nelson, 1961.

Unger, Merrill F. *Biblical Demonology*. Chicago: Scripture Press, 1965.

——. *Demons in the World Today*. Wheaton, IL: Tyndale House, 1971.

Discipleship

(See also Christian Life)

Borg, Marcus J. *Jesus: A New Vision: The Spirit, Society, and the Life of Discipleship*. San Francisco: Harper & Row, 1987.

Dulles, Avery. *A Church to Believe In: Discipleship and the Dynamics of Freedom*. New York: Crossroad, 1982.

*Foster, Richard J. *Celebration of Discipline*. San Francisco: Harper & Row, 1988.

Happel, Stephen, and James J. Walter. *Conversion and Discipleship: A Christian Foundation for Ethics and Doctrine*. Philadelphia: Fortress, 1986.

*Newbigin, Lesslie. *Proper Confidence: Faith, Doubt, and Certainty in Christian Discipleship*. Grand Rapids: Eerdmans, 1995.

Sire, James W. *Discipleship of the Mind*. Downers Grove: InterVarsity, 1990.

*Wilkins, Michael J. *Following the Master: Discipleship in the Steps of Jesus*. Grand Rapids: Zondervan, 1992.

Election

(See also Predestination, Salvation)

Berkouwer, G.C. *Divine Election*. English Translation. Grand Rapids: Eerdmans, 1960.

Buehlmann, Walbert. *God's Chosen Peoples*. Maryknoll, NY: Orbis Books, 1982.

Murray, John. *Calvin on Scripture and Divine Sovereignty*. Grand Rapids: Baker, 1960.

*Pinnock, Clark H., ed. *Grace Unlimited*. Minneapolis: Bethany Fellowship, Inc., 1975.

Warfield, B.B. "Election." *Selected Shorter Writings of B.B. Warfield*. Nutley, NJ: Presbyterian and Reformed Publishing, 1970-73. Pp. 285-98.

Eschatology

(See also Millennium)

*Archer, Gleason L., et al. *The Rapture: Pre-, Mid-, or Post-Tribulational?* Grand Rapids: Academie, 1984.

Beasley-Murray, George R. *Jesus and the Future*. New York: St. Martin's, 1954.

Berkouwer, G.C. *The Return of Christ*. Grand Rapids: Eerdmans, 1972.

Bultmann, Rudolf. *History and Eschatology*. Edinburgh: University Press, 1957.

Dodd, C.H. *The Coming of Christ*. Cambridge: University Press, 1951.

Dunning, H. Ray. *The Second Coming*. Kansas City: Beacon Hill, 1995.

Glasson, Thomas F. *The Second Advent*. London: Epworth, 1963.

Heim, Karl. *The World: Its Creation and Consummation*. Edinburgh: Oliver and Boyd, 1962.

Hoekema, Anthony A. *The Bible and the Future*. Grand Rapids: Eerdmans, 1979.

*Ladd, George E. *The Blessed Hope*. Grand Rapids: Eerdmans, 1956.

——. *The Presence of the Future*. Grand Rapids: Eerdmans, 1974.

Minear, Paul S. *Christian Hope and the Second Coming*. Philadelphia: Westminster, 1954.

*Moltmann, Jürgen. *The Coming of God: Christian Eschatology*. Minneapolis: Augsburg Fortress, 1996.

——. *Theology of Hope: On the Grounds and the Implications of a Christian Eschatology*. New York: Harper & Row, 1967.

Robinson, John A.T. *Jesus and His Coming*. Philadelphia: Westminster, 1979.

Schwarz, Hans. *On the Way to the Future: A Christian View of Eschatoloy in Light of Current Trends in Religion, Philosophy, and Science*. Rev. ed. Minneapolis: Augsburg, 1979.

*Travis, Stephen H. *I Believe in the Second Coming of Jesus*. Grand Rapids: Eerdmans, 1982.

Vos, Geerhardus. *The Pauline Eschatology*. Grand Rapids: Baker, 1982.

Eternal Life (Immortality)

Badham, Paul. *Christian Beliefs about Life after Death.* New York: Barnes & Noble Books, 1976.

Badham, Paul, and Linda Badham. *Immortality or Extinction?* Totowa, NJ: Barnes & Noble Books, 1982.

*Baillie, John. *And the Life Everlasting*. London: Oxford University Press, 1950.

*Cullmann, Oscar. *Immortality of the Soul or Resurrection of the Dead?* London: Epworth, 1960.

*Harris, Murray J. *Raised Immortal: Resurrection and Immortality in the New Testament*. Grand Rapids: Eerdmans, 1983.

Hick, John. *Death and Eternal Life.* New York: Harper & Row, 1976.

*Küng, Hans. *Eternal Life?*. Garden City, NY: Doubleday, 1984.

Martin-Achard, Robert. *From Death to Life.* Edinburgh: Oliver and Boyd, 1960.

Moody, Dale. *The Hope of Glory.* Grand Rapids: Eerdmans, 1964.

Moore, Clifford H. *Ancient Beliefs in the Immortality of the Soul.* New York: Cooper Square, 1963.

Pelikan, Jaroslav. *The Shape of Death: Life, Death, and Immortality in the Early Fathers.* New York: Abingdon, 1961.

Ethics (See Moral Theology)

Evangelism

Ferm, Robert O. *Cooperative Evangelism.* Grand Rapids: Zondervan, 1958.

Green, Michael. *Evangelism in the Early Church*. Grand Rapids: Eerdmans, 1970.

Hoekstra, Harvey T. *Evangelism in Eclipse: World Mission and the World Council of Churches*. Exeter: Paternoster, 1979.

McGrath, Alister E. *Explaining Your Faith*. Grand Rapids: Zondervan, 1989.

Moberg, David O. *The Great Reversal: Evangelism and Social Concern*. Philadelphia: Lippincott, 1977.

Morgenthaler, Sally. *Worship Evangelism*. Grand Rapids: Zondervan, 1995.

*Packer, James I. *Evangelism and the Sovereignty of God*. Downers Grove: InterVarsity, 1961.

Pannell, William. *Evangelism from the Bottom Up*. Grand Rapids: Zondervan, 1991.

*Salter, Darius. *American Evangelism: Its Theology and Practice*. Wheaton, IL: BridgePoint, 1996.

Stott, John R.W. *Fundamentalism and Evangelism*. Grand Rapids: Eerdmans, 1959.

*Watson, David. *I Believe in Evangelism*. Grand Rapids: Eerdmans, 1977.

Evil

(See also Theodicy)

Ahern, M.B. *The Problem of Evil*. New York: Schocken Books, 1971.

*Davis, Stephen T., ed. *Encountering Evil: Live Options in Theodicy*. Atlanta: John Knox, 1981.

Farley, Edward. *Good and Evil: Interpreting a Human Condition*. Minneapolis: Fortress, 1990.

*Feinberg, John S. *The Many Faces of Evil: Theological Systems and the Problem of Evil*. Grand Rapids: Zondervan, 1994.

——. *Theologies and Evil*. Washington, DC: University Press of America, 1979.

Geisler, Norman L. *The Roots of Evil*. Grand Rapids: Zondervan, 1981.

Griffin, David R. *Evil Revisited: Responses and Considerations*. Albany: State University of New York Press, 1991.

*Hick, John. *Evil and the God of Love*. New York: Harper & Row, 1978.

Joad, C.E.M. *God and Evil*. London: Faber and Faber Limited, 1942.

Madden, Edward, and Peter Hare. *Evil and the Concept of God*. Springfield, IL: C.C. Thomas, 1968.

Maritain, Jacques. *God and the Permission of Evil*. Milwaukee: Bruce Publishing, 1966.

Ricoeur, Paul. *The Symbolism of Evil*. Boston: Beacon, 1967.

Faith

*Baillie, Donald M. *Faith in God and its Christian Consummation*. Edinburgh: T. & T. Clark, 1927.

*Berkhof, Hendrikus. *Christian Faith: An Introduction to the Study of Faith*. Grand Rapids: Eerdmans, 1986.

Berkouwer, G.C. *Faith and Justification*. Grand Rapids: Eerdmans, 1954.

Bevan, Edwyn. R. *Symbolism and Belief*. Boston: Beacon, 1957.

*Dillenberger, John. *Contours of Faith*. Nashville: Abingdon, 1969.

Ebeling, Gerhard. *The Nature of Faith*. London: Collins, 1961.

*Fowler, James W. *Stages of Faith: The Psychology of Human Development and the Quest for Meaning*. San Francisco: Harper & Row, 1981.

Hick, John. *Faith and Knowledge*. Ithaca, NY: Cornell University Press, 1966.

Maclaren, Elizabeth. *The Nature of Belief*. New York: Hawthorn Books, 1976.

Smith, W. Cantwell. *Faith and Belief*. Princeton, NJ: Princeton University Press, 1979.

*Stokes, Kenneth. *Faith Is a Verb: Dynamics of Adult Faith Development*. Mystic, CT: Twenty-Third Publications, 1992.

Tillich, Paul. *The Dynamics of Faith*. New York: Harper & Row, 1958.

Forgiveness

(See also Repentance, Salvation)

Brakenhielm, Carl R. *Forgiveness*. Minneapolis: Fortress, 1993.

*Donnelly, Doris. *Learning to Forgive*. Nashville: Abingdon, 1982.

Emerson, James G. *Dynamics of Forgiveness*. Philadelphia: Westminster, 1964.

*Jones, L. Gregory. *Embodying Forgiveness: A Theological Analysis*. Grand Rapids: Eerdmans, 1995.

Klassen, William. *The Forgiving Community*. Philadelphia: Westminster, 1966.

*Oden, Thomas C. *Corrective Love: The Power of Communion Discipline*. St. Louis: Concordia, 1995.

God

*Bavinck, Herman. *The Doctrine of God*. Grand Rapids: Eerdmans, 1951.

Brunner, Emil. *The Christian Doctrine of God*. London: Lutterworth, 1949.

Fiorenza, Elisabeth S. *In Memory of Her*. New York: Crossroads, 1983.

Jüngel, Eberhard *God as the Mystery of the World*. Grand Rapids: Eerdmans, 1983

Kasper, Walter. *The God of Jesus Christ*. New York: Crossroad, 1985.

Kaufman, Gordon D. *God the Problem*. Cambridge, MA: Harvard University Press, 1972.

——. *The Theological Imagination: Constructing the Concept of God*. Philadelphia: Westminster, 1981.

Kenny, Anthony J.P. *The God of the Philosophers*. New York: Oxford University Press, 1979.

King, Robert H. *The Meaning of God*. London: SCM, 1974.

McFague, Sallie. *Models of God: Theology for an Ecological Nuclear Age*. London: SCM, 1987.

*Niebuhr, H. Richard. *Radical Montheism and Western Culture*. Louisville: Westminster/John Knox, 1993.

*Oden, Thomas C. *The Living God*. Systematic Theology: Volume One. San Francisco: Harper San Francisco, 1987.

Ogden, Schubert M. *The Reality of God*. New York: Harper & Row, 1966.

Owen, H.P. *Christian Theism: A Study in its Basic Principles*. Edinburgh: T. & T. Clark, 1984.

——. *Concepts of Deity*. New York: Herder and Herder, 1971.

Scharlemann, Robert P. *The Being of God: Theology and the Experience of Truth*. New York: Seabury, 1981.

Ward, Keith. *The Concept of God*. Oxford: Blackwell, 1974.

Wijk-Bos, Johanna W.H. van. *Reimagining God: The Case for Scriptural Diversity*. Louisville: Westminster/John Knox, 1995.

God: Attributes of God

Anderson, Ray S. *Historical Transcendence and the Reality of God: A Christological Critique*. Grand Rapids: Eerdmans, 1975.

Birch, L. Charles. *The Nature and God*. London: SCM, 1965.

*Bloesch, Donald G. *God the Almighty: Power, Wisdom, Holiness, Love*. Downers Grove: InterVarsity, 1995.

*Boice, James M. *The Sovereign God*. Downers Grove: InterVarsity, 1978.

Charnock, Stephen. *The Existence and Attributes of God*. Ann Arbor, MI: Kregel Publishing, 1958.

Creel, Richard E. *Divine Impassibility: An Essay in Philosophical Theology*. New York: Cambridge University Press, 1986.

Daane, James. *The Freedom of God*. Grand Rapids: Eerdmans, 1973.

Dorner, Isaak A. *Divine Immutability*. Minneapolis: Fortress, 1994.

Hartshorne, Charles. *Omnipotence and Other Theological Mistakes*. Albany, NY: State University of New York, 1984.

Neville, Robert C. *God the Creator: On the Transcendence and Presence of God*. Chicago: University of Chicago Press, 1968.

Newlands, George M. *Theology of the Love of God*. London: Collins, 1980.

Placher, William C. *The Domestication of Transcendence: How Modern Thinking About God Went Wrong*. Louisville: Westminster/John Knox, 1996.

*Plantinga, Alvin. *God, Freedom, and Evil*. Grand Rapids: Eerdmans, 1974.

*Pinnock, Clark, et al. *The Openness of God*. Downers Grove: InterVarsity, 1994.

Raschke, Carl A., and Susan D. Raschke. *The Engendering God: Male and Female Faces of God*. Louisville: Westminster/John Knox, 1995.

Rupp, E. Gordon. *The Righteousness of God*. London: Hodder and Stoughton, 1953.

*Tozer, A.W. *Knowledge of the Holy: The Attributes of God, Their Meaning in the Christian Life*. New York: Harper & Row, 1961.

God: Trinity

Fortman, Edmund J. *The Triune God*. Philadelphia: Westminster, 1972.

Hill, William J. *The Three-Personed God*. Washington, DC: University Press of America, 1983.

Jenson, Robert W. *The Triune Identity*. Philadelphia: Fortress, 1982.

Jüngel, Eberhard. *The Doctrine of the Trinity*. Grand Rapids: Eerdmans, 1976.

*LaCugna, Catherine M. *God for Us: The Trinity and Christian Life*. New York: HarperCollins, 1991.

Lee, Jung Young. *The Trinity in Asian Perspective*. Nashville: Abingdon, 1996.

Lowry, Charles W. *The Trinity and Christian Devotion*. London: Eyre and Spottiswoode, 1946.

Mackey, James P. *The Christian Experience of God as Trinity*. London: SCM, 1983.

*McGrath, Alister E. *Understanding the Trinity*. Grand Rapids: Academie Books, 1988.

*Moltmann, Jürgen. *The Trinity and the Kingdom: The Doctrine of God*. San Francisco: Harper & Row, 1981.

Rahner, Karl. *The Trinity*. New York: Herder and Herder, 1970.

Richardson, Cyril. *The Doctrine of the Trinity*. New York: Abingdon, 1958.

Toon, Peter, and James D. Spiceland. *One God in Trinity*. Westchester, IL: Cornerstone Books, 1980.

Wainwright, Arthur W. *The Trinity in the New Testament*. London: SPCK, 1962.

Welch, Claude. *In This Name: The Doctrine of the Trinity in Contemporary Theology*. New York: Scribner's, 1952.

God: Existence of God

Barnes, Jonathan. *The Ontological Argument*. New York: St. Martin's, 1972.

Craig, William L. *The Cosmological Argument from Plato to Leibniz*. New York: Barnes and Noble Books, 1980.

Hartshorne, Charles. *Anselm's Discovery: A Re-Examination of the Ontological Proof for God's Existence*. La Salle, IL: Open Court, 1965.

Hick, John, ed. *The Existence of God*. New York: Macmillan, 1964.

*Küng, Hans. *Does God Exist?: An Answer for Today*. Garden City, NY: Doubleday, 1980.

Maritain, Jacques. *Approaches to God*. New York: Harper, 1954.

Matson, Wallace I. *The Existence of God*. Ithaca, NY: Cornell University, 1965.

McPherson, Thomas. *The Argument from Design*. New York: St. Martin's, 1972.

Owen, H.P. *The Moral Argument for Christian Theism*. London: Allen & Unwin, 1965.

*Plantinga, Alvin, ed. *The Ontological Argument*. Garden City, NY: Anchor Books, 1965.

Rowe, William L. *The Cosmological Argument*. Princeton: Princeton University Press, 1975.

*Swinburne, Richard. *The Existence of God*. New York: Oxford University Press, 1979.

God: Knowableness of God

*Baillie, John. *Our Knowledge of God*. New York: Scribner's, 1939.

*——. *The Sense of the Presence of God*. New York: Scribner's, 1962.

Cotton, James H. *Christian Knowledge of God*. New York: Macmillan, 1951.

*Gill, Jerry H. *On Knowing God*. Philadelphia: Westminster, 1981.

Hardy, Daniel W. *Praising and Knowing God*. Philadelphia: Westminster, 1985.

Haymes, Brian. *The Concept of the Knowledge of God*. New York: Macmillan, 1988.

Hazelton, R. *Knowing the Living God*. Valley Forge: Judson, 1969.

Lossky, Vladimir. *The Vision of God*. Clayton, WI: American Orthodox Press, 1963.

Owen, H.P. *The Christian Knowledge of God*. London: Athlone, 1969.

*Packer, James I. *Knowing God*. London: Hodder and Stoughton, 1973.

*Trueblood, D. Elton. *The Knowledge of God*. New York: Harper & Brothers, 1939.

Gospel (See Law and Gospel)

Grace

Boff, Leonardo. *Liberating Grace*. Maryknoll, NY: Orbis Books, 1979.

Chafer, Lewis S. *Grace*. Grand Rapids: Zondervan, 1922.

Fransen, Piet. *The New Life of Grace*. New York: Paulist, 1979.

Haight, Roger. *The Experience and Language of Grace*. New York: Paulist, 1979.

Moeller, Charles, and Gérard Philips. *The Theology of Grace and the Oecumenical Movement*. London: Mowbray, 1961.

*Moffatt, James. *Grace in the New Testament*. New York: R. Long & R.R. Smith, 1932.

*Oden, Thomas C. *The Transforming Power of Grace*. Nashville: Abingdon, 1993.

Rondet, Henri. *The Grace of Christ*. Philadelphia: Westminster, 1966.

Torrance, Thomas F. *The Doctrine of Grace in the Apostolic Fathers*. Edinburgh: Oliver and Boyd, 1948.

Van Til, Cornelius. *Common Grace and the Gospel*. Nutley, NJ: Presbyterian and Reformed Publishing, 1974.

Watson, Phillip S. *The Concept of Grace*. Philadelphia: Muhlenberg, 1959.

Williams, Norman P. *The Grace of God*. London: Hodder & Stoughton, 1966.

Heaven

(See also Hell)

Church, F. Forrester. *Entertaining Angels: A Guide to Heaven for Atheists and True Believers*. San Francisco: Harper & Row, 1987.

*Iersel, Bas van, and Edward Schillebeeckx, eds. *Heaven*. New York: Seabury, 1979.

Kreeft, Peter. *Heaven: The Heart's Deepest Longing*. Cambridge: Harper & Row, 1980.

*Simon, Ulrich E. *Heaven in the Christian Tradition*. New York: Harper, 1958.

Smith, Wilbur M. *The Biblical Doctrine of Heaven*. Chicago: Moody, 1968.

Hell

(See also Heaven)

*Crockett, William V., et al. *Four Views on Hell*. Grand Rapids: Zondervan, 1992.

Dixon, Larry. *The Other Side of the Good News: Confronting Contemporary Challenges to Jesus' Teaching on Hell*. Wheaton, IL: Victor, 1992.

Rowell, Geoffrey. *Hell and the Victorians*. Oxford: Clarendon, 1974.

Walker, Daniel P. *The Decline of Hell*. Chicago: University of Chicago Press, 1964.

*Walls, Jerry L. *Hell: The Logic of Damnation*. Notre Dame: Notre Dame University Press, 1992.

Holiness (See God: Attributes of God, Sanctification)

Holy Spirit (Pneumatology)

*Barrett, C.K. *The Holy Spirit and the Gospel Tradition*. London: SPCK, 1966.

Berkhof, Hendrikus. *Doctrine of the Holy Spirit*. Atlanta: John Knox, 1964.

Bruner, Frederick D. *A Theology of the Holy Spirit*. Grand Rapids: Eerdmans, 1970.

Congar, Yves. *I Believe in the Holy Spirit*. 3 vols. New York: Seabury, 1983.

*Dunn, James D.G. *Jesus and the Spirit*. London: SCM, 1975.

Ewert, David. *The Holy Spirit in the New Testament*. Scottdale, PA: Herald, 1983.

*Green, Michael. *I Believe in the Holy Spirit*. Grand Rapids: Eerdmans, 1989.

Griffith-Thomas, W.H. *The Holy Spirit of God*. Grand Rapids: Eerdmans, 1955.

Hendry, George S. *The Holy Spirit in Christian Theology*. Philadelphia: Westminster, 1965.

Heron, Alisdair I.C. *The Holy Spirit*. Philadelphia: Westminster, 1983.

Hopko, Thomas. *The Spirit of God*. Wilton, CT: Morehouse-Barlow, 1976.

*Horton, Stanley M. *What the Bible Says About the Holy Spirit*. Springfield, MO: Gospel Publishing House, 1976.

Lampe, Geoffrey W.H. *God as Spirit*. Oxford: Clarendon, 1977.

Moltmann, Jürgen. *The Spirit of Life*. Minneapolis: Fortress, 1992.

Montague, George T. *The Holy Spirit: Growth of a Biblical Tradition.* New York: Paulist, 1976.

*Morris, Leon. *Spirit of the Living God*. Chicago: InterVarsity, 1960.

Moule, Charles F.D. *The Holy Spirit*. Grand Rapids: Eerdmans, 1978.

*Oden Thomas C. *Life in the Spirit*. Systematic Theology: Volume Three. San Francisco: Harper San Francisco, 1992.

Ramsey, Michael. *Holy Spirit: A Biblical Study*. London: SPCK, 1977.

Ryrie, Charles C. *The Holy Spirit*. Chicago: Moody, 1965.

Schweizer, Eduard. *The Holy Spirit*. Philadelphia: Fortress, 1980.

Thielicke, Helmut. *Theology of Spirit*. Grand Rapids: Eerdmans, 1982.

Walvoord, John F. *The Holy Spirit*. Grand Rapids: Zondervan, 1954.

Holy Spirit: Attributes of the Holy Spirit

*Agnew, Milton S. *The Holy Spirit: Friend and Counselor*. Kansas City: Beacon Hill, 1980.

Boer, Harry R. *Pentecost and Missions*. Grand Rapids: Eerdmans, 1961.

*Deere, Jack. *Surprised by the Power of the Spirit*. Grand Rapids: Zondervan, 1993.

Gunkel, Hermann. *The Influence of the Holy Spirit*. Philadelphia: Fortress, 1979.

Kuyper, Abraham. *The Work of the Holy Spirit*. Grand Rapids: Eerdmans, 1956.

Opsahl, Paul D., ed. *The Holy Spirit in the Life of the Church*. Minneapolis: Augsburg, 1978.

Robinson, Henry W. *The Christian Experience of the Holy Spirit*. London: Nisbet, 1928.

Smail, Thomas M. *Reflected Glory: The Spirit in Christ and Christians.* Grand Rapids: Eerdmans, 1976.

Tayler, John V. *The Go-Between God: The Holy Spirit and the Christian Mission.* New York: Oxford University Press, 1979.

Williams, Donald T. *The Person and Work of the Holy Spirit.* Nashville: Broadman & Holman, 1994.

Holy Spirit: Holy Spirit Baptism and Gifts

Bridge, Donald, and David Phypers. *Spiritual Gifts and the Church.* Downers Grove: InterVarsity, 1973.

Christenson, Larry. *Speaking in Tongues and Its Significance for the Church.* Minneapolis: Bethany Fellowship, 1968.

*Dunn, James D. G. *Baptism in the Holy Spirit.* Philadelphia: Westminster, 1977.

Greathouse, William M. *The Fullness of the Spirit.* Kansas City: Beacon Hill, 1958.

Griffiths, Michael. *Grace-Gifts.* Grand Rapids: Eerdmans, 1979.

Hoekema, Anthony A. *Holy Spirit Baptism.* Grand Rapids: Eerdmans, 1972.

——. *Tongues and Spirit Baptism.* Grand Rapids: Baker 1981.

Horton, Wade H., ed. *The Glossolalia Phenomenon.* Cleveland, TN: Pathway, 1966.

Lloyd-Jones, D. Martyn. *The Baptism and Gifts of the Spirit.* Grand Rapids: Baker, 1996.

Mills, Watson E. *Speaking in Tongues: A Guide to Research on Glossolalia.* Grand Rapids: Eerdmans, 1986.

Purkiser, W.T. *The Gifts of the Spirit.* Kansas City: Beacon Hill, 1975.

Schep, J.A. *Spirit Baptism and Tongue Speaking According to Scripture.* Grand Rapids: Eerdmans, 1970.

*Stott, John R.W. *Baptism and Fullness of the Holy Spirit*. Downers Grove: InterVarsity, 1974.

Taylor, Richard S. *What Does It Mean to Be Filled With the Spirit?* Kansas City: Beacon Hill, 1995.

Unger, Merrill F. *The Baptism and Gifts of the Holy Spirit*. Chicago: Moody, 1974.

*Williams, J. Rodman. *The Gift of the Holy Spirit Today*. Plainfield, NJ: Logos International, 1980.

Hope

Alves, Rubem A. *A Theology of Human Hope*. Washington, DC: Corpus Books, 1969.

Bloch, Ernst. *The Future of Hope*. Ed. Walter H. Capps. Philadelphia: Fortress, 1970.

Brunner, Emil. *Eternal Hope*. London: Lutterworth, 1954.

Cousins, Ewert H., ed. *Hope and the Future of Man*. Philadelphia: Fortress, 1972.

Hebblethwaite, Brian. *The Christian Hope*. Grand Rapids: Eerdmans, 1985.

Marcel, Gabriel. *Fresh Hope for the World*. London: Longmans, 1960.

*Moltmann, Jürgen. *Theology of Hope: On the Grounds and the Implications of a Christian Eschatology*. New York: Harper & Row, 1967.

Moody, Dale. *The Hope of Glory*. Grand Rapids: Eerdmans, 1964.

*Travis, Stephen H. *Christian Hope and the Future of Man*. Downers Grove: InterVarsity, 1980.

Humanity (Anthropology)

Babbage, Stuart B. *Man in Nature and Grace*. Grand Rapids: Eerdmans, 1957.

Cairns, David S. *The Image of God in Man*. New York: Philosophical Library, 1953.

Carey, George. *I Believe in Man*. Grand Rapids: Eerdmans, 1977.

Clark, Gordon H. *A Christian View of Men and Things*. Grand Rapids: Eerdmans, 1952.

Eichrodt, Walther. *Man in the Old Testament*. London: SCM, 1959.

Hefner, Philip. *The Human Factor: Evolution, Culture, and Religion*. Minneapolis: Augsburg Fortress, 1993.

*Kümmel, Werner G. *Man in the New Testament*. London: Epworth, 1963.

Laidlaw, John. *The Bible Doctrine of Man*. Edinburgh: T. & T. Clark, 1905.

Machen, John G. *The Christian View of Man*. New York: Macmillan, 1937.

*Moltmann, Jürgen. *Man: Christian Anthropology in the Conflicts of the Present*. London: SPCK, 1974.

*Niebuhr, Reinhold. *The Nature and Destiny of Man*. New York: Scribner's, 1949.

*Pannenberg, Wolfhart. *Anthropology in Theological Perspective*. Philadelphia: Westminster, 1985.

Robinson, Henry W. *The Christian Doctrine of Man*. Edinburgh: T. & T. Clark, 1926.

Smith, Charles R. *The Bible Doctrine of Man*. London: Epworth, 1951.

Stacey, David. *The Pauline View of Man*. New York: St. Martin's, 1956.

Wolff, Hans W. *The Anthropology of the Old Testament*. Philadelphia: Fortress, 1981.

Humanity: Human Attributes

*Berkouwer, G.C. *Man: The Image of God*. Grand Rapids: Eerdmans, 1962.

*Brunner, Emil. *Man in Revolt*. London: R.T.S. Lutterworth, 1962.

Davis, Charles. *Body as Spirit*. New York: Seabury, 1976.

Hardy, Alister. *The Spiritual Nature of Man*. New York: Oxford University, 1979.

Hoekema, Anthony A. *Created in God's Image: The Christian Doctrine of Man*. Grand Rapids: Eerdmans, 1986.

*Owen, D.R.G. *Body and Soul: A Study on the Christian View of Man*. Philadelphia: Westminster, 1956.

Robinson, John A.T. *The Body: A Study in Pauline Theology*. London: SCM, 1952.

Shedd, Russell F. *Man in Community*. London: Epworth, 1958.

Wright, J.S. *Man in the Process of Time: A Christian Assessment of the Powers and Functions of Human Personality*. Grand Rapids: Eerdmans, 1956.

Humanity: Human Freedom

*Basinger, David, and Randall Basinger, eds. *Predestination and Free Will: Four Views of Divine Sovereignty and Human Freedom*. Downers Grove: InterVarsity, 1986.

Bay, Christian. *The Structure of Freedom*. Stanford, CA: Stanford University Press, 1958.

*Edwards, Jonathan. *Freedom of the Will*. Indianapolis: Bobbs-Merrill, 1969.

*Erasmus, Desiderius, and Martin Luther. *Discourse on Free Will*. New York: Frederick Ungar, 1960.

Käsemann, Ernst. *Jesus Means Freedom*. Philadelphia: Fortress, 1969.

*Kemp, Eric W., ed. *Man Fallen and Free*. London: Hodder & Stoughton, 1969.

Pannenberg, Wolfhart. *The Idea of God and Human Freedom*. Philadelphia: Westminster, 1973.

Richardson, Peter. *Paul's Ethic of Freedom*. Philadelphia: Westminster, 1979.

Zagzebski, Linda T. *The Dilemma of Freedom and Foreknowledge*. New York: Oxford University Press, 1991.

Humanity: Gender and Sexuality

(See also Women)

Clark, Stephen B. *Man and Woman in Christ*. Ann Arbor, MI: Servant Books, 1980.

Cook, Kaye, and Lance Lee. *Man and Woman: Alone and Together*. Wheaton, IL: Victor, 1992.

Gallagher, Charles A., et al. *Embodied in Love: Sacramental Spirituality and Sexual Intimacy*. New York: Crossroad, 1985.

Genovesi, Vincent J. *In Pursuit of Love: Catholic Morality and Human Sexuality*. Wilmington, DE: M. Glazier, 1987.

Hurley, James B. *Man and Woman in Biblical Perspective*. Grand Rapids: Zondervan, 1981.

*Jewett, Paul K. *Man as Male and Female*. Grand Rapids: Eerdmans, 1975.

Keller, Catherine. *From a Broken Web: Separation, Sexism, and Self*. Boston: Beacon, 1986.

Mollenkott, Virginia R. *Women, Men, and the Bible*. New York: Crossroad, 1988.

Nelson, James B. *Body Theology*. Louisville: Westminster/John Knox, 1992.

——. *Embodiment: An Approach to Sexuality and Christian Theology*. Minneapolis: Augsburg, 1978.

Nelson, James B., and Sandra P. Longfellow, eds. *Sexuality and the Sacred: Sources for Theological Reflection*. Louisville: Westminster/John Knox, 1994.

*Sayers, Dorothy L. *Are Women Human?* Grand Rapids: Eerdmans, 1971.

*Stafford, Tim. *Sexual Chaos*. Downers Grove: InterVarsity, 1993.

Trible, Phyllis. *God and the Rhetoric of Sexuality*. Philadelphia: Fortress, 1978.

Van Leeuwen, Mary S. *Gender and Grace*. Downers Grove: InterVarsity, 1990.

Jesus Christ (Christology)

Bonhoeffer, Dietrich. *Christology*. London: Collins, 1966.

Cobb, Jr., John B. *Christ in a Pluralistic Age*. Philadelphia: Westminster, 1975.

*Cullmann, Oscar. *The Christology of the New Testament*. Philadelphia: Westminster, 1959.

*Dunn, James D.G. *Christology in the Making*. Philadelphia: Westminster, 1980.

*Fuller, Reginald H. *The Foundations of New Testament Christology*. New York: Scribner's, 1965.

*Grillmeier, Aloys, with Theresia Hainthaler. *Christ in Christian Tradition*. 2 vols in 4. Louisville: Westminster/John Knox, 1975-1995.

*Henry, Carl F.H. *The Identity of Jesus of Nazareth*. Nashville: Broadman & Holman, 1992.

Hopkins, Julie M. *Towards a Feminist Christology*. Grand Rapids: Eerdmans, 1995.

Longenecker, Richard N. *The Christology of Early Jewish Christianity*. Naperville, IL: A.R. Allenson, 1970.

*Marshall, I. Howard. *The Origins of New Testament Christology*. Downers Grove: InterVarsity, 1976.

McGrath, Alister E. *The Making of Modern German Christology, 1750-1990*. Grand Rapids: Zondervan, 1994.

*——. *Understanding Jesus*. Grand Rapids: Academie Books, 1987.

Moltmann, Jürgen. *Jesus Christ for Today's World*. Minneapolis: Fortress, 1994.

——. *The Way of Jesus Christ: Christology in Messianic Dimensions*. London: SCM, 1990.

Moule, Charles F.D. *The Origin of Christology*. New York: Cambridge University Press, 1977.

Norris, Richard A. *The Christological Controversy*. Philadelphia: Fortress, 1980.

O'Collins, Gerald. *Christology: A Biblical, Historical, and Systematic Study of Jesus Christ*. New York: Oxford University Press, 1995.

Ogden, Schubert M. *The Point of Christology*. San Francisco: Harper & Row, 1982.

*Pelikan, Jaroslav J. *Jesus Through the Centuries: His Place in the History of Culture*. New Haven, CN: Yale University Press, 1985.

Pittenger, W. Norman. *Christology Reconsidered*. London: SCM, 1970.

Relton, Herbert. *A Study in Christology*. New York: Macmillan, 1934.

*Runia, Klaas. *The Present-day Christological Debate*. Downers Grove: InterVarsity, 1984.

Schillebeeckx, Edward. *Jesus: An Experiment in Christology*. New York: Seabury, 1979.

Sobrino, Jon. *Christology at the Crossroads*. Maryknoll, NY: Orbis Books, 1978.

Jesus Christ: Attributes of Jesus Christ

*Baillie, Donald M. *God Was in Christ*. New York: Scribner's, 1948.

*Barth, Karl. *The Humanity of God*. Richmond: John Knox, 1970.

Berkouwer, G.C. *The Person of Christ*. Grand Rapids: Eerdmans, 1954.

Boff, Leonardo. *Jesus Christ, Liberator*. Maryknoll, NY: Orbis Books, 1978.

Braaten, Carl E. *Christ and Counter-Christ*. Philadelphia: Fortress, 1972.

Bruce, Alexander B. *The Humiliation of Christ*. Edinburgh: T. & T. Clark, 1895.

Bultmann, Rudolf. *Jesus and the World*. New York: Scribner's, 1934.

Cobb, Jr., John B. *Christ in a Pluralistic Age*. Philadelphia: Westminster, 1975.

Cupitt, Don. *The Debate about Christ*. London: SCM, 1979.

Frei, Hans W. *The Identity of Jesus Christ*. Philadelphia: Fortress, 1975.

Fuller, Reginald H. *The Mission and Achievement of Jesus*. London: SCM, 1954.

Hellwig, Monika K. *Jesus, the Compassion of God*. Wilmington, DE: M. Glazier, 1983.

Hengel, Martin. *The Son of God*. Philadelphia: Fortress, 1976.

Kasper, Walter. *Jesus the Christ*. New York: Paulist, 1976.

*McGrath, Alister E. *Understanding Jesus*. Grand Rapids: Academie Books, 1987.

*Moltmann, Jürgen. *The Crucified God*. London: SCM, 1974.

*——. *The Way of Jesus Christ*. San Francisco: Harper & Row, 1990.

*Oden, Thomas C. *The Word of Life*. Systematic Theology: Volume Two. San Francisco: Harper San Francisco, 1989.

Pawlikowski, John T. *Christ in the Light of the Christian-Jewish Dialogue*. New York: Paulist, 1982.

Robinson, John A.T. *The Human Face of God*. Philadelphia: Westminster, 1973.

Schillebeeckx, Edward. *Christ: The Experience of Jesus as Lord*. New York: Crossroad, 1980.

——. *Jesus: Son of God?* New York: Seabury, 1982.

Warfield, B.B. *The Person and Work of Christ*. Philadelphia: Presbyterian and Reformed Publishing, 1950.

*Wells, David F. *The Person of Christ*. Westchester, IL: Crossway Books, 1984.

*Witherington III, Ben. *Jesus the Sage: The Pilgrimage of Wisdom*. Minneapolis: Augsburg Fortress, 1994.

Jesus Christ: Incarnation

Galot, Jean. *Who is Christ?: A Theology of the Incarnation*. Chicago: Franciscan Herald, 1981.

Gore, Charles. *The Incarnation of the Son of God*. New York: C. Scribner's Sons, 1891.

Goulder, Michael D., ed. *Incarnation and Myth*. Grand Rapids: Eerdmans, 1979.

*Green, Michael, ed. *The Truth of God Incarnate*. Grand Rapids: Eerdmans, 1977.

Hebblethwaite, Brian. *The Incarnation: Collected Essays in Christology*. New York: Cambridge University Press, 1987.

Hick, John. *The Metaphor of God Incarnate: Christology in a Pluralistic Age*. Louisville: Westminster/John Knox, 1994.

Hick, John, ed. *The Myth of God Incarnate*. London: SCM, 1977.

*Pannenberg, Wolfhart. *Jesus: God and Man*. Philadelphia: Westminster, 1977.

Pittenger, W. Norman. *The Word Incarnate*. New York: Harper, 1959.

*Torrance, Thomas F. *Space, Time and Incarnation*. Grand Rapids: Eerdmans, 1976.

Jesus Christ: Historical Jesus

Aune, David E. *Jesus and the Synoptic Gospels*. Madison, WI: InterVarsity, 1980.

Bornkamm, Günther. *Jesus of Nazereth*. New York: Harper, 1960.

Bowker, John W. *Jesus and the Pharisees*. Cambridge: Cambridge University Press, 1973.

*Bruce, F.F. *Jesus and Christian Origins Outside the New Testament*. London: Hodder & Stoughton, 1984.

Bultmann, Rudolf. *Jesus Christ and Mythology*. New York: Scriber's, 1958.

Caird, George B. *Jesus and the Jewish Nation*. London: Athlone, 1965.

Crossan, John D. *The Historical Jesus: The Life of a Mediterranean Jewish Peasant*. San Francisco: Harper, 1991.

*Guthrie, Donald. *A Shorter Life of Christ*. Grand Rapids: Zondervan, 1970.

Harrison, Everett F. *A Short Life of Christ*. Grand Rapids: Eerdmans, 1968.

Harvey, Anthony E. *Jesus and the Constraints of History*. Philadelphia: Westminster, 1982.

Jeremias, Joachim. *The Problem of the Historical Jesus*. Philadelphia: Fortress, 1964.

Kähler, Martin. *The So-Called Historical Jesus and the Historic, Biblical Christ*. Philadelphia: Fortress, 1964.

Mackey, James P. *Jesus the Man and the Myth*. London: SCM, 1979.

*Marshall, I. Howard. *I Believe in the Historical Jesus*. Grand Rapids: Eerdmans, 1977.

Robinson, James M. *A New Quest of the Historical Jesus*. Naperville, IL: A. R. Allenson, 1959.

Schweitzer, Albert. *The Quest of the Historical Jesus*. Rev. ed. New York: Macmillan, 1968.

Strauss, David F. *The Life of Jesus Critically Examined*. London: SCM, 1972.

*Sykes, Stephen W., and John P. Clayton, eds. *Christ, Faith and History.* London: Cambridge University Press, 1972.

Tatum, W. Barnes. *In Quest of Jesus.* Atlanta: John Knox, 1982.

Vermes, Geza. *Jesus the Jew: A Historian's Reading of the Gospel.* 2nd ed. New York: Macmillan, 1983.

*Witherington III, Ben. *The Jesus Quest: The Third Search for the Jew of Nazareth.* Downers Grove: InterVarsity, 1995.

Ziesler, John A. *The Jesus Question.* Guilford: Lutterworth, 1980.

Jesus Christ: Virgin Birth

Boslooper, Thomas. *The Virgin Birth.* Philadelphia: Westminster, 1962.

*Brown, Raymond E. *The Birth of the Messiah.* Garden City, NY: Doubleday, 1977. Rev. ed., 1993.

——. *The Virginal Conception and Bodily Resurrection of Jesus.* New York: Paulist, 1973.

Campenhausen, Hans von. *The Virgin Birth in the Theology of the Ancient Church.* Naperville, IL: A.R. Allenson, 1964.

Edwards, Douglas A. *The Virgin Birth in History and Faith.* London: Faber & Faber, 1943.

*Machen, John G. *The Virgin Birth of Christ.* London: J. Clarke, 1958.

Jesus Christ: Resurrection

Brown, Raymond E. *The Virginal Conception and Bodily Resurrection of Jesus.* New York: Paulist, 1974.

*Davis, Stephen T. *Risen Indeed: Making Sense of the Resurrection.* Grand Rapids: Eerdmans, 1993.

*Fuller, Reginald H. *The Formation of the Resurrection Narratives*. Philadelphia: Fortress, 1980.

Gaffin, Richard B. *The Centrality of the Resurrection: A Study in Paul's Soteriology*. Grand Rapids: Baker Book House, 1978.

Habermas, Gary R. *The Resurrection of Jesus*. Grand Rapids: Baker, 1980.

Harris, Murray J. *Raised Immortal: Resurrection and Immortality in the New Testament*. Grand Rapids: Eerdmans, 1983.

*Ladd, George E. *I Believe in the Resurrection of Jesus*. Grand Rapids: Eerdmans, 1975.

Lüdemann, Gerd. *What Really Happened to Jesus: A Historical Approach to the Resurrection*. Louisville: Westminster/John Knox, 1996.

Marxsen, Willi. *The Resurrection of Jesus of Nazareth*. Philadelphia: Fortress, 1970.

*O'Collins, Gerald. *What Are They Saying About the Resurrection?* New York: Paulist, 1978.

Perkins, Pheme. *Resurrection: New Testament Witness and Contemporary Reflection*. Garden City, NY: Doubleday, 1984.

Perrin, Norman. *The Resurrection According to Matthew, Mark, and Luke*. Philadelphia: Fortress, 1977.

Ramsey, A. Michael. *The Resurrection of Christ*. Philadelphia: Westminter, 1946.

Justice

Baird, J. Arthur. *The Justice of God in the Teaching of Jesus*. Philadelphia: Westminster, 1963.

*Brunner, Emil. *Justice and the Social Order*. New York: Harper & Row, 1945.

Hollenbach, David. *Claims in Conflict: Retrieving and Renewing the Catholic Human Rights Tradition*. New York: Paulist, 1979.

*MacIntyre, Alasdair C. *Whose Justice? Which Rationality?* Notre Dame: University of Notre Dame Press, 1988.

*Niebuhr, Reinhold. *Justice and Mercy*. Louisville: Westminster/John Knox, 1991.

——. *Love and Justice: Selections from the Shorter Writings of Reinhold Niebuhr*. Ed. D.B. Robertson. Louisville: Westminster/John Knox, 1992.

Rawls, John. *A Theory of Justice*. Cambridge, MA: Belknap, 1971.

Tillich, Paul. *Love, Power, and Justice*. New York: Oxford University Press, 1954.

Will, James E. *The Universal God: Justice, Love, and Peace in the Global Village*. Louisville: Westminster/John Knox, 1994.

*Wolterstorff, Nicholas. *Until Justice and Peace Embrace*. Grand Rapids: Eerdmans, 1984.

Justification

(See also Salvation)

*Anderson, George H., et al., eds. *Justification by Faith*. Minneapolis: Augsburg, 1985.

Barth, Markus. *Justification*. Grand Rapids: Eerdmans, 1971.

Berkouwer, G.C. *Faith and Justification*. Grand Rapids: Eerdmans, 1954.

Buchanan, James. *The Doctrine of Justification*. Grand Rapids: Baker, 1955.

Forde, Gerhard O. *Justification by Faith: A Matter of Death and Life*. Ramsey, NJ: Sigler, 1991.

Küng, Hans. *Justification: The Doctrine of Karl Barth and a Catholic Reflection*. Philadelphia: Westminster, 1981.

*McGrath, Alister E. *Iustitia Dei: A History of the Christian Doctrine of Justification*. 2 vols. New York: Cambridge University Press, 1986.

*——. *Justification by Faith: What It Means for Us Today*. Grand Rapids: Zondervan, 1990.

Reumann, John H.P. *'Righteousness' in the New Testament: 'Justification' in the United States Lutheran-Roman Catholic Dialogue*, with responses by J. A. Fitzmyer and J. D. Quinn. Philadelphia: Fortress, 1982.

Ritschl, Albrecht. *Critical History of the Christian Doctrine of Justification and Reconciliation*. Edinburgh: Edmonston and Douglas, 1872.

Ziesler, John A. *The Meaning of Righteousness in Paul*. Cambridge: Cambridge University Press, 1972.

Kingdom of God

Beasley-Murray, George R. *Jesus and the Kingdom of God*. Grand Rapids: Eerdmans, 1986.

*Bright, John. *The Kingdom of God in Bible and Church*. London: Lutterworth, 1955.

Chilton, Bruce. *The Kingdom of God in the Teaching of Jesus*. Philadelphia: Fortress, 1984.

Dodd, C.H. *The Parables of the Kingdom*. New York: Scribner's, 1961.

Ellul, Jacques. *The Presence of the Kingdom*. Philadelphia: Westminster, 1951.

Glasson, Thomas F. *His Appearing and His Kingdom*. London: Epworth, 1953.

Hiers, Richard H. *The Kingdom of God in the Synoptic Tradition*. Gainesville, FL: University of Florida Press, 1970.

*Ladd, George E. *Crucial Questions About the Kingdom of God*. Grand Rapids: Eerdmans, 1966.

*——. *Jesus and the Kingdom*. Waco, TX: Word Books, 1964.

Lundström, Gösta. *The Kingdom of God in the Teaching of Jesus*. Richmond: John Knox, 1963.

*Moltmann, Jürgen. *The Trinity and the Kingdom: The Doctrine of God*. San Francisco: Harper & Row, 1981.

*Niebuhr, H. Richard. *The Kingdom of God in America*. New York: Harper, 1959.

Otto, Rudolf. *The Kingdom of God and the Son of Man*. London: Lutterworth, 1943.

Perrin, Norman. *The Kingdom of God in the Teaching of Jesus*. Philadelphia: Westminster, 1963.

Ridderbos, Herman. *The Coming of the Kingdom*. Philadelphia: Presbyterian and Reformed Publishing, 1962.

Schnackenburg, Rudolf. *God's Rule and Kingdom*. New York: Herder and Herder, 1963.

Schweitzer, Albert. *The Mytery of the Kingdom of God: The Secret of Jesus' Messiahship and Passion*. New York: Macmillan, 1950.

*Snyder, Howard A. *The Community of the King*. Downers Grove: InterVarsity, 1977.

Vos, Geerhardus. *The Teaching of Jesus Concerning the Kingdom of God and the Church*. Grand Rapids: Eerdmans, 1958.

Weiss, Johannes. *Jesus' Proclamation of the Kingdom of God*. Philadelphia: Fortress, 1971.

Law and Gospel

*Anderson, James N.D. *Morality, Law and Grace*. London: Tyndale, 1972.

Ellul, Jacques. *The Theological Foundation of Law*. New York: Doubleday, 1960.

Finnis, John. *Natural Law and Natural Rights*. New York: Oxford University Press, 1980.

Forde, Gerhard O. *The Law-Gospel Debate: An Interpretation of Its Historical Development*. Minneapolis: Augsburg, 1969.

*Fuller, Daniel P. *Gospel and Law*. Grand Rapids: Eerdmans, 1980.

*Kinghorn, Kenneth C. *The Gospel of Grace*. Nashville: Abingdon, 1992.

Mascall, E.L. *Theology and the Gospel of Christ*. London: SPCK, 1977.

*Strickland, Wayne G. *The Law, the Gospel, and the Modern Christian: Five Views*. Grand Rapids: Zondervan, 1993.

Van Til, Cornelius. *Common Grace and the Gospel*. Nutley, NJ: Presbyterian and Reformed Publishing, 1974.

Walther, Carl F.W. *God's "No" and God's "Yes": The Proper Distinction Between Law and Gospel*. Ed. W.C. Pieper. St. Louis, MO: Concordia, 1973.

*Woodbridge, John D., et al. *The Gospel in America*. Grand Rapids: Zondervan, 1979.

Liturgy

(See also Sacraments, Worship)

Botte, Bernard. *From Silence to Participation: An Insider's View of Liturgical Renewal*. Washington, DC: Pastoral, 1988.

Bouyer, Louis. *Rite and Man: Natural Sacredness and Christian Liturgy*. Notre Dame: University of Notre Dame Press, 1963.

Dix, Gregory. *The Shape of the Liturgy*. London: Dacre, 1945.

*Jones, Cheslyn, et al., eds. *The Study of Liturgy*. New York: Oxford University Press, 1978.

Kavanagh, Aidan. *On Liturgical Theology*. New York: Pueblo, 1984.

*Klausner, Theodor. *A Short History of the Western Liturgy*. New York: Oxford University Press, 1969.

Koenker, Ernest B. *The Liturgical Renaissance in the Roman Catholic Church*. Chicago: University of Chicago Press, 1954.

Schmemann, Alexander. *Introduction to Liturgical Theology*. Portland, ME: American Orthodox, 1966.

Vagaggini, Cyprian. *Theological Dimensions of the Liturgy*. Collegeville, MN: Liturgical, 1976.

Lord's Supper/Eucharist

(See also Sacraments)

Allmen, J.J. von. *The Lord's Supper*. Richmond: John Knox, 1969.

Arndt, Elmer J.F. *The Font and the Table*. Richmond: John Knox, 1967.

Balasuriya, Tissa *The Eucharist and Human Liberation*. Maryknoll, NY: Orbis Books, 1979.

Bouyer, Louis. *Eucharist*. Notre Dame: University of Notre Dame Press, 1968.

*Cullmann, Oscar, and F.J. Leenhardt. *Essays on the Lord's Supper*. Richmond: John Knox, 1958.

Duffy, Regis A. *Real Presence, Worship, Sacrament, and Commitment*. San Francisco: Harper and Row, 1982.

Hay, Leo. *Eucharist: A Thanksgiving Celebration*. Wilmington, DE: Michael Glazier, 1989.

Jeremias, Joachim. *The Eucharistic Words of Jesus*. Philadelphia: Fortress, 1977.

*Marshall, I. Howard. *Last Supper and Lord's Supper*. Grand Rapids: Eerdmans, 1981.

*Marty, Martin E. *The Lord's Supper*. Philadelphia: Fortress, 1980.

Mazza, Enrico. *The Eucharistic Prayers of the Roman Rite*. New York: Pueblo, 1986.

*Packer, James I., ed. *Eucharistic Sacrifice*. London: Church Book Room, 1962.

Power, David N. *The Eucharistic Mystery*. New York: Crossroad, 1992.

Schillebeeckx, Edward. *Christ, the Sacrament of the Encounter With God*. New York: Sheed and Ward, 1963.

Thurian, Max. *The Eucharistic Memorial*. Richmond: John Knox, 1961.

*Wainwright, Geoffrey. *Eucharist and Eschatology*. New York: Oxford University Press, 1981.

Love

d'Arcy, Martin C. *The Mind and Heart of Love*. London: Faber and Faber, 1954.

Furnish, Victor P. *The Love Command in the New Testament*. Nashville: Abingdon, 1972.

Guitton, Jean. *Human Love*. Chicago: H. Regnery, 1967.

*King, Jr., Martin Luther. *Strength to Love*. New York: Harper & Row, 1963.

Lewis, C.S. *The Four Loves*. New York: Harcourt, Brace, 1960.

McIntyre, John. *On the Love of God*. New York: Harper, 1962.

*Morris, Leon. *Testaments of Love*. Grand Rapids: Eerdmans, 1981.

*Nygren, Anders. *Agape and Eros*. London: SPCK, 1957.

Outka, Gene. *Agape: An Ethical Analysis*. New Haven: Yale University Press, 1972.

Piper, John. *Love Your Enemies*. New York: Cambridge University Press, 1979.

Spicq, Ceslas. *Agape in the New Testament*. St. Louis: B. Herder, 1963.

Williams, Daniel D. *The Spirit and the Forms of Love*. New York: Harper & Row, 1968.

Mary/Mariology

*Benko, Stephen. *Protestants, Catholics, and Mary*. Valley Forge, PA: Judson, 1968.

Carol, Juniper B. *Mariology*. Milwaukee: Bruce Publishing, 1955.

Graef, Hilda. *Mary: A History of Doctrine and Devotion*. 2 vols. New York: Sheed and Ward, 1965.

Jelly, Frederick. *Madonna: Mary in the Catholic Tradition*. Huntington, IN: Our Sunday Visitor, 1986.

*Oberman, Heiko A. *The Virgin Mary in Evangelical Perspective*. Philadelphia: Fortress, 1971.

Method, Theological

Avis, Paul D.L. *The Methods of Modern Theology*. Basingstoke: Marshall Pickering, 1986.

Chopp, Rebecca S., and Mark L. Taylor, eds. *Reconstructing Christian Theology*. Minneapolis: Fortress, 1994.

Clayton, John P. *The Concept of Correlation*. New York: W. de Gruyter, 1980.

Ebeling, Gerhard. *The Study of Theology*. Philadelphia: Fortress, 1979.

Farley, Edward. *Ecclesial Reflection: An Anatomy of Theological Method*. Philadelphia: Fortress, 1982.

Fiorenza, Francis S. *Beyond Hermeneutics: Theology as Discourse*. New York: Continuum, 1995.

Fiorenza, Francis S., and John P. Galvin, eds. *Systematic Theology*. 2 vols. Minneapolis: Fortress, 1991.

*Gadamer, Hans G. *Truth and Method*. New York: Crossroad, 1982.

Gilkey, Langdon. *Message and Existence: An Introduction to Christian Theology*. New York: Seabury, 1979.

——. *Naming the Whirlwind*. Indianapolis, IN: Bobbs-Merrill, 1969.

Haight, Roger. *Dynamics of Theology*. New York: Paulist, 1990.

Hodgson, Peter C. *Winds of the Spirit: A Constructive Christian Theology*. Louisville: Westminster/John Knox, 1994.

*Hodgson, Peter C., and Robert H. King, eds. *Christian Theology: An Introduction to Its Traditions and Tasks*. Philadelphia: Fortress, 1985.

Kaufman, Gordon D. *An Essay on Theological Method*. Missoula, MT: Scholars Press, 1975.

*Lindbeck, George A. *The Nature of Doctrine: Religion and Theology in a Post-liberal Age*. Philadelphia: Westminster, 1984.

Lints, Richard. *The Fabric of Theology: A Prolegomenon to Evangelical Theology*. Grand Rapids: Eerdmans, 1993.

Lonergan, Bernard J.F. *Method in Theology*. New York: Seabury, 1979.

*McGrath, Alister E. *The Genesis of Doctrine*. Oxford: Blackwell, 1990.

*McGrath, Alister E. *Understanding Doctrine: What It Is and Why It Matters*. Grand Rapids: Zondervan, 1992.

*Mueller, J.J. *What Are They Saying About Theological Method*? New York: Paulist, 1984.

Nygren, Anders. *Meaning and Method*. Philadelphia: Fortress, 1972.

*Pannenberg, Wolfhart. *Introduction to Systematic Theology*. Grand Rapids: Eerdmans, 1991.

*Torrance, Thomas F. *The Ground and Grammar of Theology*. Charlottesville: University Press of Virginia, 1980.

Tracy, David. *Blessed Rage for Order*. New York: Seabury, 1975.

——. *The Analogical Imagination*. New York: Crossroad, 1981.

*Woodbridge, John D., and Thomas E. McComiskey, eds. *Doing Theology in Today's World*. Grand Rapids: Zondervan, 1994.

Millennium

(See also Eschatology)

Boettner, Loraine. *The Millennium*. Philadelphia: Presbyterian and Reformed Publishing, 1958.

*Clouse, Robert G., ed. *The Meaning of the Millennium: Four Views*. Downers Grove: InterVarsity, 1977.

*Grenz, Stanley J. *The Millennial Maze*. Downers Grove: InterVarsity, 1992.

*Ladd, George E. *The Blessed Hope*. Grand Rapids: Eerdmans, 1975.

Mauro, Philip. *The Seventy Weeks and the Great Tribulation*. Boston: Hamilton Bros. Scripture Truth Depot, 1923.

Sandeen, Ernest R. *The Roots of Fundamentalism: British and American Millennarianism*. Chicago: University of Chicago Press, 1970.

Toon, Peter, ed. *Puritans, the Millennium and the Future of Israel*. Cambridge: James Clarke, 1970.

Walvoord, John F. *The Millennial Kingdom*. Findlay, OH: Dunham Publishing, 1959.

Weber, Timothy P. *Living in the Shadow of the Second Coming: American Premillennialism, 1875-1982*. New York: Oxford University Press, 1979.

West, Nathaniel. *The Thousand Years: Studies in Eschatology*. Fincastle, VA: Scripture Truth, n.d.

Ministry

(See also Church)

*Anderson, Ray S., ed. *Theological Foundations for Ministry*. Grand Rapids: Eerdmans, 1978.

*Barrett, C.K. *Church, Ministry and Sacraments in the New Testament*. Grand Rapids: Eerdmans, 1985.

*Clouse, Bonnidell, and Robert G. Clouse, eds. *Women in Ministry: Four Views*. Downers Grove: InterVarsity, 1989.

Congar, Yves. *Lay People in the Church*. Westminster, MD: Newman, 1957.

Cooke, Bernard. *Ministry to Word and Sacraments: History and Theology*. Philadelphia: Fortress, 1976.

Ford, Douglas W.C. *The Ministry of the Word*. Grand Rapids: Eerdmans, 1979.

Küng, Hans. *Why Priests?* Garden City, NY: Doubleday, 1972.

Lawler, Michael G.A. *A Theology of Ministry*. Kansas City, MO: Sheed & Ward, 1990.

Mohler, James A. *The Origin and Evolution of the Priesthood*. Staten Island, NY: Alba House, 1970.

Moore, Peter C., ed. *Bishops But What Kind?: Reflections on Episcopacy*. London: SPCK, 1982.

Neuhaus, Richard J. *Freedom for Ministry*. Grand Rapids: Eerdmans, 1992.

Osborne, Kenan B. *Ministry: Lay Ministry in the Roman Catholic Church*. New York: Paulist, 1993.

Power, David N. *Gifts That Differ: Lay Ministries Established and Unestablished*. New York: Pueblo Publishing, 1980.

Provost, James H., ed. *Code, Community, Ministry*. Washington, DC: Canon Law Society of America, 1983.

Reid, John K.S. *The Biblical Doctrine of the Ministry*. Edinburgh: Oliver and Boyd, 1955.

Rhodes, Lynn N. *Co-Creating: A Feminist Vision of Ministry*. Louisville: Westminster/John Knox, 1987.

Schillebeeckx, Edward. *The Church with a Human Face: A New and Expanded Theology of Ministry*. New York: Crossroad, 1985.

——. *Ministry: Leadership in the Community of Jesus Christ*. New York: Crossroad, 1981.

Shelp, Earl E., and Ronald Sunderland, eds. *A Biblical Basis for Ministry*. Philadelphia: Westminster, 1981.

*Stone, Bryan P. *Compassionate Ministry: Theological Foundations*. Maryknoll, NY: Orbis Books, 1996.

*Stott, John R. W. *Christian Mission in the Modern World*. Downers Grove: InterVarsity, 1975.

Swete, Henry B., ed. *Essays on the Early History of the Church and the Ministry*. London: Macmillan, 1918.

Miracles

*Brown, Colin. *Miracles and the Critical Mind*. Grand Rapids: Eerdmans, 1984.

*——. *That You May Believe: Miracles and Faith—Then and Now*. Grand Rapids: Eerdmans, 1985.

Burns, Robert M. *The Great Debate on Miracles*. Lewisburg, PA: Bucknell University Press, 1981.

Farmer, Herbert H. *Are Miracles Possible?* London: SPCK, 1960.

*Fuller, Reginald H. *Interpreting the Miracles*. London: SCM, 1963.

Geisler, Norman L. *Miracles and the Modern Mind*. Grand Rapids: Baker, 1992.

Kee, Howard C. *Medicine, Miracle, and Magic in New Testament Times*. New York: Cambridge University Press, 1986.

——. *Miracle in the Early Christian World*. New Haven: Yale University Press, 1983.

Keller, Ernst, and Marie-Luise Keller. *Miracles in Dispute*. London: SCM, 1969.

*Lewis, C.S. *Miracles*. New York: Macmillan, 1947.

Loos, Hendrik van der. *The Miracles of Jesus*. Leiden: E.J. Brill, 1965.

Monden, Louis. *Signs and Wonders: A Study of the Miraculous Element in Religion*. New York: Desclee, 1966.

Moule, Charles F.D., ed. *Miracles; Cambridge Studies in Their Philosophy and History*. London: A. R. Mowbray, 1965.

*Swinburne, Richard. *The Concept of Miracle*. New York: St. Martin's, 1970.

Theissen, Gerd. *The Miracle Stories of the Early Christian Tradition*. Edinburgh: T. & T. Clark, 1983.

Mysticism

Bancroft, Anne. *Twentieth Century Mystics and Sages*. Chicago: Regnery, 1976.

Bowman, Mary A. *Western Mysticism*. Chicago: American Library Association, 1978.

Butler, E. Cuthbert. *Western Mysticism: The Teaching of Augustine, Gregory and Bernard*. London: Constable, 1927.

*Egan, Harvey D. *What Are They Saying about Mysticism?* New York: Paulist, 1982.

Grant, Patrick. *A Dazzling Darkness: An Essay on the Experience of Prayer*. London: SPCK, 1963.

*Harkness, Georgia E. *Mysticism: Its Meaning and Message*. Nashville: Abingdon, 1973.

Hügel, Friedrich von. *The Mystical Element in Religion*. Greenwood, SC: Attic, 1961.

Inge, William R. *Christian Mysticism*. London: Methuen & Co., 1899.

Johnston, William. *Christian Mysticism Today*. San Francisco: Harper & Row, 1985.

Katz, Steven T. *Mysticism and Religious Traditions*. New York: Oxford University Press, 1983.

King, Ursula. *Towards a New Mysticism*. New York: Seabury, 1980.

Lossky, Vladimir. *The Mystical Theology of the Eastern Church*. London: J. Clarke, 1957.

Louth, Andrew. *The Origins of Christian Mystical Tradition*. New York: Oxford University Press, 1981.

Petry, Ray C., ed. *Late Medieval Mysticism*. Philadelphia: Westminster, 1957.

*Underhill, Evelyn. *Mysticism*. New York: One World Publishing, 1993.

Zaehner, Robert C. *Mysticism, Sacred and Profane*. Oxford: Clarendon Press, 1957.

Natural Theology (See Revelation: General Revelation)

Power

Bainbridge, William S. *Satan's Power: A Deviant Psychotherapy Cult*. Berkeley: University of California Press, 1978.

*Caird, George B. *Principalities and Powers*. Oxford: Clarendon, 1956.

Chopp, Rebecca S. *The Power to Speak: Feminism, Language, God*. New York: Crossroad, 1989.

Cone, James H. *Black Theology and Black Power*. San Francisco: Harper & Row, 1989.

Haroutunian, Joseph. *The Lust for Power*. New York: Scribner's Sons, 1949.

McDonnell, Kilian, ed. *The Holy Spirit and Power: The Catholic Charismatic Renewal*. Garden City, NY: Doubleday, 1975.

Russell, Jeffrey B. *The Prince of Darkness: Radical Evil and the Power of Good in History*. Ithaca, NY: Cornell University Press, 1988.

*Schlier, Heinrich. *Principalities and Powers in the New Testament*. Edinburgh: Nelson, 1961.

Tillich, Paul. *Love, Power, and Justice*. New York: Oxford University Press, 1954.

Vieth, Richard F. *Holy Power, Human Pain*. Bloomington, IN: Meyer-Stone Books, 1988.

*Yinger, J. Milton. *Religion in the Struggle for Power*. Durham, NC: Duke University Press, 1946.

Prayer

Barth, Karl. *Prayer*. 2nd ed. Ed. Don E. Saliers. Philadelphia: Westminster, 1985.

*Bloesch, Donald G. *The Struggle of Prayer*. New York: Harper & Row, 1980.

*Ellul, Jacques. *Prayer and Modern Man*. New York: Seabury, 1970.

Forsyth, Peter T. *The Soul of Prayer*. London: C.H. Kelly, 1916.

*Foster, Richard. *Prayer*. San Francisco: HarperSanFrancisco, 1992.

Heiler, Frederick. *Prayer: A Study in the History and Psychology of Religion*. New York: Oxford University Press, 1958.

Palmer, Benjamin M. *Theology of Prayer*. Richmond: John Knox, 1984.

Vogel, Arthur A. *God, Prayer, and Healing: Living With God in a World Like Ours*. Grand Rapids: Eerdmans, 1995.

Predestination

(See also Election, Salvation)

*Basinger, David, and Randall Basinger, eds. *Predestination and Free Will: Four Views of Divine Sovereignty and Human Freedom.* Downers Grove: InterVarsity, 1986.

Boettner, Loraine. *The Reformed Doctrine of Predestination*. Grand Rapids: Eerdmans, 1941.

*Calvin, John. *Concerning the Eternal Predestination of God.* Greenwood, SC: Attic, 1961.

Murray, John. *Calvin on Scripture and Divine Sovereignty*. Grand Rapids: Baker, 1960.

*Pinnock, Clark., ed. *Grace Unlimited*. Minneapolis: Bethany Fellowship, Inc., 1975.

Prophecy

Allis, Oswald T. *Prophecy and the Church*. Philadelphia: The Presbyterian and Reformed Publishing, 1945.

Blenkinsopp, Joseph. *Prophecy and Canon*. Notre Dame: University of Notre Dame Press, 1977.

*Ellis, Edward E. *Prophecy and Hermeneutic in Early Christianity*. Tübingen: Mohr, 1978.

*Pate, Marvin, and Calvin Haines. *Doomsday Delusions*. Downers Grove: InterVarsity, 1995.

Walvoord, John F. *Major Bible Prophecies*. Grand Rapids: Zondervan, 1991.

——. *The Nations, Israel and the Church in Prophecy*. Grand Rapids: Zondervan, 1988.

Providence

Berkouwer, G.C. *The Providence of God*. Grand Rapids: Eerdmans, 1952.

*Helm, Paul. *The Providence of God*. Downers Grove: InterVarsity, 1994.

Langford, M.J. *Providence*. London: SCM, 1981.

Pollard, William. G. *Chance and Providence*. New York: Scribner's, 1958.

*Thomas, Owen, ed. *God's Activity in the World*. Chico, CA: Scholars Press, 1983.

Wiles, Maurice, ed. *Providence.* London: SPCK, 1969.

Regeneration (New Birth)

(See also Salvation, Sanctification)

*Burkhardt, Helmut. *The Biblical Doctrine of Regeneration.* Downers Grove: InterVarsity, 1978.

Citron, Bernhard. *New Birth: A Study of the Evangelical Doctrine of Conversion in the Protestant Fathers.* Edinburgh: University Press, 1951.

*Hewitt, Glenn A. *Regeneration and Morality.* Brooklyn: Carlson, 1991.

Winchester, Olive May. *Crisis Experiences in the Greek New Testament.* Kansas City: Beacon Hill, 1953.

Repentance

(See also Conversion, Forgiveness, Salvation)

*Chamberlain, William D. *The Meaning of Repentance.* Philadelphia: Westminster, 1943.

Donnelly, Doris. *Repentance and Reconciliation in the Church.* Ed. Michael J. Henchal. Collegeville, MN: Litergical Press, 1987.

*Grider, J. Kenneth. *Repentance Unto Life: What It Means to Repent.* Kansas City: Beacon Hill, 1965.

Schlink, Basilea. *Repentance.* Minneapolis: Bethany House, 1984.

Stokes, Bob. *Repentance, Revival, and the Holy Spirit.* Chicago: Moody, 1975.

Watson, Thomas. *The Doctrine of Repentance.* Carlisle, PA: Banner of Truth, 1987.

Resurrection

(See also Jesus Christ—Resurrection)

Cavallin, Hans C.C. *Life After Death: Paul's Argument for the Resurrection of the Dead*. Lund: Gleerup, 1974.

*Evans, Christopher F. *Resurrection and the New Testament*. London: SCM, 1970.

Künneth, Walter. *The Theology of the Resurrection*. London: SCM, 1965.

Léon-Dufour, Xavier. *Resurrection and the Message of Easter*. New York: Holt, Rinehart and Winston, 1974.

Marxsen, Willi. *The Significance of the Message of the Resurrection for Faith in Jesus Christ*. Ed. Charles F.D. Moule. London: SCM, 1968.

*O'Donovan, Oliver. *Resurrection and Moral Order*. Grand Rapids: Eerdmans, 1986.

Schep, J.A. *The Nature of the Resurrection Body*. Grand Rapids: Eerdmans, 1964.

Selby, Peter. *Look for the Living: The Corporate Nature of Resurrection Faith*. Philadelphia: Fortress, 1976.

Williams, Rowan. *Resurrection*. London: Darton, Longman and Todd, 1982.

Revelation

Baillie, John. *The Idea of Revelation in Recent Thought*. New York: Columbia University Press, 1956.

Brunner, Emil. *Revelation and Reason*. Philadelphia: Westminster, 1947.

*Dulles, Avery. *Models of Revelation*. Garden City, NY: Doubleday, 1983.

Henry, Carl. F.H. *God, Revelation, and Authority.* 6 vols. Waco, TX.: Word Books, 1979-1983.

McDonald, Hugh D. *Ideas of Revelation, An Historical Study (1700-1860).* New York: St. Martin's, 1959.

*——. *Theories of Revelation.* Grand Rapids: Baker, 1979.

*Niebuhr, H. Richard. *The Meaning of Revelation.* New York: Macmillan, 1960.

*Pannenberg, Wolfhart, ed. *Revelation as History.* New York: Macmillan, 1969.

Schillebeeckx, Edward. *Revelation and Theology.* New York: Sheed and Ward, 1967.

Shorter, Aylward. *Revelation and Its Interpretation.* London: Geoffry Chapman, 1983.

Revelation: General Revelation (Natural Theology)

(See also God-Existence of God)

*Barth, Karl, and Emil Brunner. *Natural Theology: Comprising "Nature and Grace by E. Brunner and the reply "No!" by K. Barth.* London: Centenary, 1946.

*Berkouwer, G.C. *General Revelation.* Grand Rapids: Eerdmans, 1955.

Cleobury, F.H. *A Return to Natural Theology.* London: Clarke, 1967.

Cobb, Jr., John B. *A Christian Natural Theology.* Philadelphia: Westminster, 1965.

*Demarest, Bruce A. *General Revelation, Historical Views and Contemporary Issues.* Grand Rapids: Zondervan, 1982.

Holloway, Maurice R. *An Introduction to Natural Theology.* New York: Appleton-Century-Crofts, 1959.

Mascall, E.L. *The Openness of Being*. London: Darton, Longman and Todd, 1971.

Revelation: Special Revelation

*Henry, Carl F.H., ed. *Revelation and the Bible: Contemporary Evangelical Thought*. Grand Rapids: Baker Book House, 1967.

Orr, James. *Revelation and Inspiration*. Grand Rapids: Eerdmans, 1952.

*Pinnock, Clark. *Biblical Revelation, The Foundation of Christian Theology*. Phillipsburg, NJ: Presbyterian and Reformed Publishing, 1985.

Warfield, B.B. *Revelation and Inspiration*. New York: Oxford University Press, 1927.

Sacraments/Sacramental Theology

(See also Baptism, Liturgy, Lord's Supper/Eucharist, Worship)

*Baillie, Donald M. *The Theology of the Sacraments*. New York: Scribner's, 1957.

*Barrett, C.K. *Church, Ministry and Sacraments in the New Testament*. Grand Rapids: Eerdmans, 1985.

Berkouwer, G.C. *The Sacraments*. Grand Rapids: Eerdmans, 1969.

Clark, Neville. *An Approach to the Theology of the Sacraments*. Chicago: Allenson, 1957.

Cooke, Bernard. *Ministry to Word and Sacrament*. Philadelphia: Fortress, 1976.

*Farmer, David H., ed. *The New Dictionary of Sacramental Worship*. Collegeville, MN: Liturgical, 1990.

Forsyth, Peter T. *The Church and the Sacraments*. London: Independent, 1953.

James, Edwin O. *Sacrifice and Sacrament*. London: Thames & Hudson, 1962.

Jenson, Robert W. *Visible Words: The Interpretation and Practice of Christian Sacraments*. Philadelphia: Fortress, 1978.

Leeming, Bernard. *The Principles of Sacramental Theology*. Westminster, MD: Newman, 1957.

Rahner, Karl. *The Church and the Sacraments*. New York: Herder and Herder, 1963.

Schillebeeckx, Edward. *Christ the Sacrament of Encounter with God*. New York: Sheed and Ward, 1963.

Staples, Rob L. *Outward Sign and Inward Grace*. Kansas City: Beacon Hill, 1991.

*Thurian, Max, and Geoffrey Wainwright. *Baptism and Eucharist: Ecumenical Convergence in Celebration*. Grand Rapids: Eerdmans, 1983.

Vorgrimler, Herbert. *Sacramental Theology*. Collegeville, MN: Liturgical, 1992.

*White, James F. *Sacraments As God's Self-Giving*. Nashville: Abingdon, 1983.

Salvation (Soteriology)

(See also Assurance, Atonement, Conversion, Election, Forgiveness, Justification, Predestination, Regeneration, Repentance, Sanctification)

*Cullmann, Oscar. *Salvation in History*. London: SCM, 1967.

*Edwards, Denis. *What Are They Saying About Salvation?* New York: Paulist, 1986.

Erickson, Millard J. *How Shall They Be Saved? The Destiny of Those Who Do Not Hear of Jesus*. Grand Rapids: Baker, 1996.

*Fackre, Gabriel, et al. *What About Those Who Have Never Heard?* Downers Grove: InterVarsity, 1995.

Fiddes, Paul S. *Past Event and Present Salvation*. Louisville: Westminster/John Knox, 1989.

Kevan, Ernest F. *Salvation*. Grand Rapids: Baker, 1963.

Kuiper, Herman. *By Grace Alone: A Study in Soteriology*. Grand Rapids: Eerdmans, 1955.

Mackintosh, H.R. *Christian Experience of Forgiveness*. London: Collins, 1961.

Murray, John. *Redemption Accomplished and Applied*. Grand Rapids: Eerdmans, 1955.

Simon, Ulrich E. *Theology of Salvation*. London: SPCK, 1953.

Taylor, Vincent. *Forgiveness and Reconciliation*. 1948 rpt.; New York: St. Martin's, 1960.

*Wells, David F. *The Search for Salvation*. Downers Grove: InterVarsity, 1978.

Sanctification (Holiness)

(See also Regeneration, Salvation)

*Alexander, Donald L., ed. *Christian Spirituality*. Downers Grove: InterVarsity, 1988.

Berkouwer, G.C. *Faith and Sanctification*. Grand Rapids: Eerdmans, 1952.

Borg, Marcus. *Conflict, Holiness and Politics in the Teachings of Jesus*. Lewiston, NY: Mellen, 1984.

*Dieter, Melvin, et al. *Five Views on Sanctification*. Grand Rapids: Academie for Zondervan, 1987.

Flew, R. Newton. *The Idea of Perfection in Christian Theology*. London: Oxford University Press, 1934.

Forsyth, Peter T. *Christian Perfection*. London: Hodder and Stoughton, 1899.

Grider, J. Kenneth. *Entire Sanctification*. Kansas City: Beacon Hill, 1980.

Neill, Stephen. *Christian Holiness*. New York: Harper, 1960.

Peterson, David. *Possessed by God*. Grand Rapids: Eerdmans, 1995.

Purkiser, W.T. *Conflicting Concepts of Holiness*. Rev. ed. Kansas City: Beacon Hill, 1972.

*Taylor, Richard S. *Exploring Christian Holiness: The Theological Formulation*. 3 vols. Kansas City: Beacon Hill, 1983-1985.

——. *Life in the Spirit: Christian Holiness in Doctrine, Experience, and Life*. Beacon Hill, 1966.

*Turner, George A. *The Vision Which Transforms*. Kansas City: Beacon Hill, 1964.

Satan (See Devil/Demons)

Scripture (See Bible)

Sin (Hamartiology)

*Berkouwer, G.C. *Sin*. Grand Rapids: Eerdmans, 1971.

McKenzie, John G. *Guilt: Its Meaning and Significance*. London: Allen & Unwin, 1962.

*Niebuhr. Reinhold. *Moral Man and Immoral Society*. New York: C. Scribner's Sons, 1948.

*Plantinga, Jr., Cornelius. *Not the Way It's Supposed to Be: A Breviary of Sin*. Grand Rapids: Eerdmans, 1995.

Rondet, Henri. *Original Sin*. Staten Island, NY: Alba House, 1972.

Schoonenberg, Peter. *Man and Sin*. Notre Dame: University of Notre Dame Press, 1965.

Smith, Charles R. *The Bible Doctrine of Sin*. London: Epworth, 1953.

*Smith, David L. *With Willful Intent: A Theology of Sin*. Wheaton, IL: Victor, 1994.

*Taylor, Richard S. *A Right Concept of Sin*. Kansas City: Beacon Hill, 1945.

Telfer, William. *The Forgiveness of Sins: An Essay in the History of Christian Doctrine and Practice*. London: SCM, 1959.

Tennant, Frederick R. *The Origin and Propagation of Sin*. Cambridge: Cambridge University Press, 1906.

——. *The Sources of the Doctrines of the Fall and Original Sin*. New York: Schocken Books, 1968.

Space (See Time and Space)

Spirituality

*Alexander, Donald L., et al. *Christian Spirituality*. Downers Grove: InterVarsity, 1988.

*Bell, Richard H., and Barbara Battin, eds. *Seeds of the Spirit: Wisdom of the Twentieth Century*. Louisville: Westminster/John Knox, 1995.

Bouyer, Louis, et. al. *A History of Christian Spirituality*. 3 vols. London: Burns & Oates, 1969.

Dupré, Louis, and Don Saliers, eds. *Christian Spirituality: Post-Reformation and Modern*. New York: Crossroad, 1989.

Griffin, David R. *Spirituality and Society: Postmodern Visions*. Albany: State University of New York Press, 1988.

Gutiérrez, Gustavo. *We Drink from Our Own Wells: The Spiritual Journey of a People*. Maryknoll, NY: Orbis Books, 1984.

Holmes, Urban T. *A History of Christian Spirituality*. New York: Seabury, 1980.

*Jones, Cheslyn, Geoffrey Wainwright and Edward Yarnold. *The Study of Spirituality*. New York: Oxford University Press, 1986.

*Lovelace, Richard. *Dynamics of Spiritual Life*. Downers Grove: InterVarsity, 1979.

McGrath, Alister E. *Roots that Refresh: A Celebration of Reformation Spirituality*. London: Hodder & Stoughton, 1991.

*——. *Spirituality in an Age of Change*. Grand Rapids: Zondervan, 1994.

Merton, Thomas. *New Seeds of Contemplation*. Norfolk, CN: New Directions, 1961.

*——. *Thomas Merton, Spiritual Master: The Essential Writings*. Ed. Lawrence S. Cunningham. New York: Paulist Press, 1992.

Packer, James I. *Keep in Step with the Spirit*. Old Tappan, NJ: Revell, 1984.

*Pannenberg, Wolfhart. *Christian Spirituality*. Philadelphia: Westminster, 1983.

Pourrat, Pierre. *Christian Spirituality*. 4 vols. London: Burns, Oates and Washbourne, 1922.

Rupp, E. Gordon. *Christian Spirituality*. Ed. P. Brooks. London: SCM, 1975.

Senn, Frank C., ed. *Protestant Spiritual Traditions*. New York: Paulist, 1986.

Sobrino, Jon. *Spirituality of Liberation*. Maryknoll, NY: Orbis Books, 1988.

Soelle, Dorothee. *On Earth as in Heaven: A Liberation Spirituality of Sharing*. Louisville: Westminster/John Knox, 1993.

Thompson, Marjorie. *Soul Feast: An Invitation to the Christian Spiritual Life*. Louisville: Westminster/John Knox, 1995.

Tugwell, Simon. *Ways of Imperfection: An Exploration of Christian Spirituality*. London: Darton, Longman, and Todd, 1984.

Wakefield, Gordon S., ed. *A Dictionary of Christian Spirituality*. Philadelphia: Westminster, 1983.

Williams, Rowan. *The Wound of Knowledge: Christian Spirituality from the New Testament to St. John of the Cross*. Cambridge, MA: Cowley Publications, 1991.

Suffering

(See also Theodicy)

Boesak, Allan. *Comfort and Protest: Reflections on the Apocalypse of John of Patmos*. Philadelphia: Westminster, 1987.

*Bonhoeffer, Dietrich. *Letters and Papers from Prison*. New York: Macmillan, 1962.

Bowker, John W. *Problems of Suffering in Religions of the World*. Cambridge: Cambridge University Press, 1970.

Gutiérrez, Gustavo. *On Job: God-Talk and the Suffering of the Innocent*. Maryknoll, NY: Orbis Books, 1987.

Kitamori, Kazoh. *Theology of the Pain of God*. Richmond: John Knox, 1965.

*Lewis, C.S. *The Problem of Pain*. New York: Macmillan, 1961.

*Soelle, Dorothee. *Suffering*. Philadelphia: Fortress, 1975.

Vieth, Richard F. *Holy Power, Human Pain*. Bloomington, IN: Meyer-Stone Books, 1988.

*Yancey, Philip. *Disappointment with God: Three Questions No One Asks Aloud*. New York: Harper Paperbacks, 1988.

Theodicy

(See also Evil, Suffering)

*Blocher, Henri. *Evil and the Cross*. Downers Grove: InterVarsity, 1994.

*Davis, Stephen T., ed. *Encountering Evil: Live Options in Theodicy*. Atlanta: John Knox, 1981.

Farley, Wendy. *Tragic Vision and Divine Compassion: A Contemporary Theodicy*. Louisville: Westminster/John Knox, 1990.

Farrer, Austin M. *Love Almighty and Ills Unlimited*. Garden City, NY: Doubleday, 1961.

Feinberg, John S. *Theologies and Evil*. Washington, DC: University Press of America, 1979.

Griffin, David R. *God, Power, and Evil: A Process Theodicy*. Philadelphia: Westminster, 1976.

*Hick, John. *Evil and the God of Love*. New York: Harper & Row, 1978.

*Lewis, C.S. *The Problem of Pain*. New York: Macmillan, 1961.

Maritain, Jacques. *God and the Permission of Evil*. Milwaukee: Bruce Publishing, 1966.

Time and Space

Alexander, Samuel. *Space, Time, and Deity*. 2 vols. London: Macmillan, 1927.

*Barr, James. *Biblical Words for Time*. Naperville, IL: A.R. Allenson, 1962.

*Cullmann, Oscar. *Christ and Time*. Philadelphia: Westminster, 1964.

*Hasker, William. *God, Time, and Knowledge*. Ithaca: Cornell University Press, 1989.

*Padgett, Alan. *God, Eternity, and the Nature of Time*. New York: St. Martin's, 1992.

Pike, Nelson. *God and Timelessness*. London: Routledge & K. Paul, 1970.

Tillich, Paul. *The Eternal Now*. New York: Scribner's, 1963.

*Torrance, Thomas F. *Space, Time, and Incarnation*. Grand Rapids: Eerdmans, 1976.

Virtue

Adeney, Bernard T. *Strange Virtues*. Downers Grove: InterVarsity, 1995.

Billington, James H. *Virtue, Public and Private*. Grand Rapids: Eerdmans, 1986.

Farley, Benjamin W. *In Praise of Virtue: An Exploration of the Biblical Virtues in a Christian Context*. Grand Rapids: Eerdmans, 1995.

*Geach, Peter T. *The Virtues*. Cambridge: Cambridge University Press, 1977.

Halberstam, Joshua. *Virtues and Values: An Introduction to Ethics*. Englewood Cliffs, NJ: Prentice Hall, 1988.

*Hauerwas, Stanley. *Character and the Christian Life*. San Antonio: Trinity University Press, 1975.

MacIntyre, Alasdair C. *After Virtue: A Study in Moral Theory*. Notre Dame: University of Notre Dame, 1981.

Slote, Michael A. *From Morality to Virtue*. New York: Oxford University Press, 1992.

Women

(See also Feminist Theology, Humanity-Gender and Sexuality)

*Bloesch, Donald G. *Is the Bible Sexist?* Westchester, IL: Crossway Books, 1982.

Brock, Rita N., et al., eds. *Setting the Table: Women in Theological Conversation*. St. Louis: Chalice, 1995.

Bushnell, Katherine C. *God's Word to Women*. Peoria, IL: Bernice Menold, 1983.

Carr, Anne E. *Transforming Grace: Christian Tradition and Women's Experience*. San Francisco: Harper & Row, 1988.

*Clouse, Bonnidell, and Robert G. Clouse, eds. *Women in Ministry: Four Views*. Downers Grove: InterVarsity, 1989.

Daniélou, Jean. *The Ministry of Women in the Early Church*. New York: Morehouse-Barlow, 1961.

Deen, Edith. *Great Women of the Christian Faith*. New York: Harper & Row, 1959.

*Evans, Mary J. *Woman in the Bible*. Downers Grove: InterVarsity, 1984.

Foh, Susan T. *Women and the Word of God*. Grand Rapids: Baker Book House, 1980.

*Malcolm, Kari T. *Women at the Crossroads*. Downers Grove: InterVarsity, 1982.

Mickelsen, Alvera. *Women, Authority and the Bible*. Downers Grove: InterVarsity, 1986.

Purvis, Sally A. *The Stained-Glass Ceiling: Churches and Their Women Pastors*. Louisville: Westminster/John Knox, 1995.

Tavard, George H. *Woman in Christian Tradition*. Notre Dame: University of Notre Dame Press, 1973.

Tucker, Ruth A. *Women in the Maze*. Downers Grove: InterVarsity, 1992.

*Tucker, Ruth A., and Walter L. Liefeld. *Daughters of the Church: Women and Ministry from New Testament Times to the Present*. Grand Rapids: Zondervan, 1987.

Vos, Clarence J. *Woman in Old Testament Worship*. Delft: Judels & Brinkman, 1968.

Williams, Don. *The Apostle Paul and Women in the Church*. Glendale, CA: Regal Books Division, 1978.

*Witherington III, Ben. *Women in the Ministry of Jesus*. New York: Cambridge University Press, 1984.

Worship

(See also Liturgy, Sacraments)

Abba, Raymond. *Principles of Christian Worship*. New York: Oxford University Press, 1957.

Allmen, J.J. von. *Worship: Its Theology and Practice*. New York: Oxford University Press, 1965.

Brunner, Peter. *Worship in the Name of Jesus*. St. Louis: Concordia, 1968.

*Cullmann, Oscar. *Early Christian Worship*. London: SCM, 1953.

*Davies, John G., ed. *The New Westminster Dictionary of Liturgy and Worship*. Philadelphia: Westminster, 1986.

Erickson, Craig D. *Participating in Worship: History, Theory, and Practice*. Louisville: Westminster/John Knox, 1989.

Hahn, William T. *Worship and Congregation*. Richmond: John Knox, 1963.

*Liesch, Barry. *People in the Presence of God: Models and Directions for Worship*. Grand Rapids: Zondervan, 1988.

*Martin, Ralph P. *Worship in the Early Church*. Grand Rapids: Eerdmans, 1975.

*——. *The Worship of God*. Grand Rapids: Eerdmans, 1982.

Micklem, Nathaniel. *Christian Worship: Studies in its History and Meaning*. London: Oxford University Press, 1959.

Power, David N. *Worship: Culture and Theology*. Washington, DC: Pastoral, 1990.

Senn, Frank C. *Christian Worship and Its Cultural Setting*. Philadelphia: Fortress, 1983.

*Underhill, Evelyn. *Worship*. New York: Harper, 1957.

*Wainwright, Geoffrey. *Doxology: A Systematic Theology*. New York: Oxford University, 1980.

*Webber, Robert. *Worship Old and New*. Rev. ed. Grand Rapids: Zondervan, 1994.

White, James F. *Introduction to Christian Worship*. Nashville: Abingdon, 1990.

THEOLOGICAL TRADITIONS

The best place to learn about the historic traditions of Christian theology is in the original and ongoing writings of each tradition. Some of them can be found in the section on Notable Theologians.

This bibliography provides mostly overviews of historic theological traditions, which come from both outside as well as inside the tradition. As such the bibliography should be used as an introductory resource for further investigation.

Eastern Orthodox Theology

Benz, Ernst. *The Eastern Orthodox Church: Its Thought and Life.* Chicago: Aldine Publishing, 1963.

Bulgakov, Sergei N. *The Orthodox Church.* Crestwood, NY: St. Vladimir's Seminary Press, 1988.

Calian, Carnegie S. *Theology Without Boundaries: Encounters of Eastern Orthodoxy and Western Tradition.* Louisville: Westminster/John Knox, 1992.

*Clendenin, Daniel B. *Eastern Orthodox Christianity: A Western Perspective.* Grand Rapids: Baker, 1994.

Florovsky, Georges. *Bible, Church, Tradition: An Eastern Orthodox View.* Belmont, MA: Nordland Publishing, 1972.

——. *Creation and Redemption.* Belmont, MA: Nordland Publishing, 1976.

*Lossky, Vladimir. *The Mystical Theology of the Eastern Church.* London: J. Clarke, 1957.

*——. *Orthodox Theology: An Introduction.* Crestwood, NY: St. Vladimir's Seminary Press, 1989.

Meyndorff, John. *Byzantine Theology.* New York: Fordham University Press, 1974.

Payne, Robert. *The Holy Fire: The Story of the Fathers of the Eastern Church*. New York: Harper, 1957.

Roberson, Ronald G. *The Eastern Christian Churches*. Rome: Pontificium Institutum Studiorum Orientalium, 1990.

Staniloae, Dumitru. *Theology and the Church*. Crestwood, NY: St. Vladimir's Seminary Press, 1980.

*Tsirpanlis, Constantine N. *Introduction to Eastern Patristic Thought and Orthodox Theology*. Collegeville, MN: Liturgical Press, 1991.

*Ware, Kallistos. *The Orthodox Way*. Crestwood, NY: St. Vladimir's Seminary Press, 1979.

*——. *The Orthodox Church*. New York: Penguin Books, 1993.

Protestant Theology

Barth, Karl. *Protestant Theology in the Nineteenth Century*. London: SCM, 1972.

Brauer, Jerald C. *Protestantism in America*. Philadelphia: Westminster, 1965.

Brown, Robert McAfee. *The Spirit of Protestantism*. New York: Oxford University Press, 1961.

*Dillenberger, John, and Claude Welch. *Protestant Christianity Interpreted Through Its Development*. New York: Macmillan, 1988.

Forell, George W. *The Protestant Faith*. Englewood Cliffs, NJ: Prentice-Hall, 1960.

Gollwitzer, Helmut. *An Introduction to Protestant Theology*. Philadelphia, Westminster, 1982.

Heron, Alasdair I.C. *A Century of Protestant Theology*. Philadelphia: Westminster, 1980.

*Marty, Martin E. *Protestantism*. New York: Holt, Rinehart and Winston, 1972.

*McGrath, Alister E. *Reformation Thought*. Oxford: Blackwell, 1988.

Tillich, Paul. *The Protestant Era*. Chicago: University of Chicago Press, 1957.

Welch, Claude. *Protestant Thought in the Nineteenth Century*. 2 vols. New Haven: Yale University Press, 1972-1985.

Whale, John S. *The Protestant Tradition*. Cambridge: Cambridge University Press, 1955.

Zahrnt, Heinz. *The Question of God: Protestant Theology in the Twentieth Century*. London: Collins, 1969.

Protestant Theology: Adventist Theology

*Damsteegt, P. Gerard. *Foundations of the Seventh-day Adventist Message and Mission*. Grand Rapids: Eerdmans, 1977.

*Froom, L. Edwin. *The Prophetic Faith of Our Fathers*, 4 vols. Washington, DC: Review and Herald Publishing, 1946-54.

*Land, Gary, ed. *Adventism in America: A History*. Grand Rapids: Eerdmans, 1986.

Nichol, Francis D. *The Midnight Cry*. Washington, DC: Review and Herald Publishing, 1945.

Paxton, Geoffrey. *The Shaking of Adventism*. Wilmington, DE: Zenith Publishers, 1977.

Protestant Theology: Anabaptist Theology

Armour, Rollin S. *Anabaptist Baptism*. Scottdale, PA: Herald, 1966.

Bender, Harold S. *The Anabaptist Vision*. Scottdale, PA: Herald, 1944.

Estep, William R. *The Anabaptist Story*. Nashville: Broadman, 1963.

*Friedmann, Robert. *The Theology of Anabaptism*. Scottdale, PA: Herald, 1973.

Hillerbrand, Hans J., ed. *A Bibliography of Anabaptism*. St. Louis: Center for Reformation Research, 1975.

*Klaassen, Walter, ed. *Anabaptism in Outline*. Scottdale, PA: Herald, 1981.

*Lienhard, Marc, ed. *The Origins and Characteristics of Anabaptism*. The Hague: Nijhoff, 1977.

Stayer, James M. *Anabaptists and the Sword*. Lawrence, KS: Coronado, 1973.

Williams, George H., and Angel Mergal, eds. *Spiritual and Anabaptist Writers*. The Library of Christian Classics. Eds. John Baillie, et al. London: SCM, 1957.

Protestant Theology: Anglican/Episcopalian Theology

Benton, Angelo A., ed. *The Church Cyclopaedia: A Dictionary of Church Doctrine, History, Organization, and Ritual Designed Especially for the Use of the Laity of the Protestant Episcopal Church in the United States of America*. 1883 rpt.; Detroit: Gale Research, 1975.

Carter, Charles S. *The English Church and the Reformation*. New York: Longmans, Green and Co., 1925.

Marshall, Michael. *The Gospel Connection*. Harrisburg: Morehouse, 1990.

*More, Paul E., and Frank L. Cross, eds. *Anglicanism*. London: SPCK, 1962.

*Neill, Stephen. *Anglicanism*. Baltimore: Penguin Books, 1965.

*Sykes, Stephen W. *The Integrity of Anglicanism*. New York: Seabury, 1978.

*Sykes, Stephen W, and John E. Booty, eds. *The Study of Anglicanism.* Philadelphia: Fortress, 1988.

Williams, Alwyn T.P. *The Anglican Tradition in the Life of England.* London: SCM, 1947.

Protestant Theology: Baptist Theology

*Armstrong, Orland K., and Marjorie M. Armstrong. *The Baptists in America.* Garden City, NY: Doubleday, 1979.

Basden, Paul A., and David S. Dockery, eds. *The People of God: Essays on the Believers' Church.* Nashville: Broadman & Holman, 1991.

Clements, Keith W., ed. *Baptists in the Twentieth Century.* London: Baptist Historical Society, 1983.

Crosby, Thomas. *The History of the English Baptists.* 4 vols. Lafayette, TN: Church History, Research and Archives, 1978.

*Dockery, David S., and Robison B. James, eds. *Beyond the Impasse?* Nashville: Broadman, 1992.

Frost, J.M., ed. *Baptist: Why and Why Not?* Nashville: Broadman & Holman, 1996.

*George, Timothy, and David S. Dockery, eds. *Baptist Theologians.* Nashville: Broadman, 1990.

Hudson, Winthrop S. *Baptists in Transition.* Valley Forge, PA: Judson, 1979.

*Leonard, Bill J. *Dictionary of Baptists in America.* Downers Grove: InterVarsity, 1994.

Lumpkin, William L. *Baptist Confessions of Faith.* Valley Forge, PA: Judson, 1969.

Payne, Ernest A. *The Baptist Union: A Short History.* London: Carey Kingsgate, 1959.

Robinson, Henry W. *Baptist Principles*. London: Carey Kingsgate, 1945.

Torbet, Robert G. *A History of the Baptists*. Valley Forge, PA: Judson, 1973.

Protestant Theology: Dispensational Theology

Bass, Clarence B. *Backgrounds to Dispensationalism*. Grand Rapids: Baker, 1977.

*Blaising, Craig, and Darrell Bock. *Progressive Dispensationalism*. Wheaton, IL: BridgePoint, 1993.

*——. *Dipensationalism, Israel and the Church: The Search for Definition*. Grand Rapids: Zondervan, 1992.

Kraus, C. Norman. *Dispensationalism in America*. Richmond: John Knox, 1958.

Ryrie, Charles C. *Dispensationalism Today*. Chicago: Moody, 1965.

*Saucy, Robert L. *The Case for Progressive Dispensationalism: The Interface Between Dispensational and Non-dispensational Theology*. Grand Rapids: Zondervan, 1993.

Protestant Theology: Friends (Quaker) Theology

Bacon, Margaret H. *The Quiet Rebels*. Philadelphia: New Society Publishers, 1985.

Barbour, Hugh. *The Quakers*. New York: Greenwood Press, 1988.

Barclay, Robert. *Barclay's Apology in Modern English*. Ed. Dean Freiday. Alburtis, PA: Hemlock, 1967.

Braithwaite, William C. *The Beginnings of Quakerism*. Cambridge: Cambridge University Press, 1955.

——. *The Second Period of Quakerism*. Cambridge: Cambridge University Press, 1961.

Brinton, Howard H. *The Religious Philosophy of Quakerism*. Wallingford, PA: Pendle Hill Publications, 1973.

Jones, Rufus M. *Quakerism: A Spiritual Movement*. Philadelphia: Meeting of Friends, 1963.

Loukes, Harold. *The Quaker Contribution*. New York: Macmillan, 1965.

*Trueblood, D. Elton. *The People Called Quakers*. New York: Harper & Row, 1966.

Williams, Walter R. *The Rich Heritage of Quakerism*. Grand Rapids: Eerdmans, 1962.

Protestant Theology: Lutheran Theology

*Althaus, Paul. *Theology of Martin Luther*. Minneapolis: Fortress, 1996.

Altmann, Walter. *Luther and Liberation*. Minneapolis: Fortress, 1992.

*Braaten, Carl E. *Principles of Lutheran Theology*. Minneapolis: Fortress, 1983.

Elert, Werner. *Structure of Lutheranism*. St. Louis, MO: Concordia, 1962.

*Gritsch, Eric W., and Robert W. Jenson. *Lutheranism*. Philadelphia: Fortress, 1976.

Gustafson, David A. *Lutherans in Crisis*. Minneapolis: Fortress, 1993.

Lazareth, William, and Péri Rasolondraibe. *Lutheran Identity and Mission*. Minneapolis: Fortress, 1994.

*Lohse, Bernhard. *Martin Luther*. Philadelphia: Fortress, 1986.

*Marty, Martin E. *Lutheranism*. Royal Oak, MI: Cathedral Publishers, 1975.

Nelson, E. Clifford., ed. *The Lutherans in North America.* Philadelphia: Fortress, 1980.

Preus, Robert D. *The Theology of Post-Reformation Lutheranism.* 2 vols. St. Louis, MO: Concordia, 1972.

Protestant Theology: Pentecostal and Charismatic Theology

*Bennett, Dennis J. *The Holy Spirit and You*. Plainfield, NJ: Logos International, 1971.

Bloch-Hoell, Nils. *The Pentecostal Movement: Its Origin, Development and Character*. New York: Humanities, 1964.

*Burgess, Stanley M., and Gary B. McGee, eds. *Dictionary of Pentecostal and Charismatic Movements*. Grand Rapids: Zondervan, 1988.

Glazier, Stephen D. *Perspective on Pentecostalism*. Washington, DC: University Press of America, 1980.

Hamilton, Michael, P. *The Charismatic Movement*. Grand Rapids: Eerdmans, 1975.

*Hollenweger, Walter J. *The Pentecostals*. Peabody, MA: Hendrickson, 1988.

McDonnell, Kilian, ed. *The Holy Spirit and Power: The Catholic Charismatic Renewal*. Garden City, NY: Doubleday, 1975.

*——. *Presence, Power, Praise: Documents on the Charismatic Renewal*. 3 vols. Collegeville, MN: Liturgical, 1980.

Nichol, John Thomas. *Pentecostalism.* New York: Harper & Row, 1966.

Poloma, Margaret M. *The Charismatic Movement*. Boston: Twayne Publishers, 1982.

Synan, Vinson, ed. *Aspects of Pentecostal-Charismatic Origins.* Plainfield, NJ: Logos International: 1975.

Sullivan, Francis A. *Charisms and Charismatic Renewal*. Ann Arbor, MI: Servant Books, 1982.

*Williams, J. Rodman. *Renewal Theology*. 3 vols. Grand Rapids: Zondervan, 1988-1992.

Protestant Theology: Pietist Theology

*Bloesch, Donald G. *The Evangelical Renaissance*. Grand Rapids: Eerdmans, 1973.

*Brown, Dale W. *Understanding Pietism*. Rev. ed. Nappanee, IN: Evangel, 1996.

Contemporary Perspectives on Pietism: A Symposium. Co-sponsored by North Park Theological Seminary and the Pietism Section of the American Academy of Religion. Chicago: Covenant, 1976.

Ellingsen, Mark. *The Evangelical Movement*. Minneapolis: Augsburg, 1988.

Grünberg, Paul. *Philipp Jakob Spener*. 3 vols. 1893-1906 rpt.; New York: Georg Olms Verlag, 1988.

*Stoeffler, F. Ernest. *The Rise of Evangelical Pietism*. Leiden: E.J. Brill, 1965.

Wakefield, Gordon S. *Puritan Devotion: Its Place in the Development of Christian Piety*. London: Epworth, 1957.

Protestant Theology: Reformed (Calvinist) Theology

Barth, Karl. *The Theology of John Calvin*. Grand Rapids: Eerdmans, 1995.

Bratt, John H. *Rise and Development of Calvinism*. Grand Rapids: Eerdmans, 1964.

Dowey, Edward A. *The Knowledge of God in Calvin's Theology*. Grand Rapids: Eerdmans, 1994.

George, Timothy. *Theology of the Reformers*. Nashville: Broadman & Holman, 1987.

Harkness, Georgia E. *John Calvin, the Man and His Ethics*. New York: H. Holt, 1931.

Hunt, George L., ed. *Calvinism and the Political Order*. Philadelphia: Westminster, 1965.

Keesecker, William F., ed. *A Calvin Treasury*. Louisville: Westminster/John Knox, 1963.

*Leith, John H. *Basic Christian Doctrine: A Summary of Christian Faith - Catholic, Protestant, and Reformed*. Louisville: Westminster/John Knox, 1992.

*——. *Introduction to the Reformed Tradition*. Louisville: Westminster/John Knox, 1980.

*McKim, Donald K., ed. *Encyclopedia of the Reformed Faith*. Louisville: Westminster/John Knox, 1992.

*McNeill, John T. *The History and Character of Calvinism*. New York: Oxford University Press, 1954.

Niesel, Wilhelm. *The Theology of Calvin*. Phiadelphia: Westminster, 1956.

Ottati, Douglas F. *Reforming Protestantism*. Louisville: Westminster/John Knox, 1995.

Parker, Thomas H.L. *Calvin: An Introduction to His Thought*. Louisville: Westminster/John Knox, 1995.

Steele, David N., and Curtis C. Thomas. *The Five Points of Calvinism: Defined, Defended, Documented*. Phillipsburg, NJ: Presbyterian & Reformed Publishing, 1963.

Wendel, François *Calvin: The Origins and Development of His Religious Thought*. New York: Harper & Row, 1963.

Protestant Theology: Wesleyan Theology

Callen, Barry L. *God As Loving Grace*. Nappanee, IN: Evangel, 1996.

Carter, Charles W., ed. *A Contemporary Wesleyan Theology: Biblical, Systematic, and Practical*. Grand Rapids: Zondervan, 1983.

Cobb, Jr., John B. *Grace and Responsibility: A Wesleyan Theology for Today*. Nashville: Abingdon, 1995.

Collins, Kenneth J. *Wesley on Salvation*. Grand Rapids: Zondervan, 1989.

Davies, Rupert E. *Methodism*. London: Epworth, 1976.

Dunning, H. Ray. *Grace, Faith, and Holiness: A Systematic Theology*. Kansas City: Beacon Hill, 1988.

Grider, J. Kenneth. *A Wesleyan-Holiness Theology*. Kansas City: Beacon Hill, 1994.

Langford, Thomas A. *Practical Divinity: Theology in the Wesleyan Tradition*. Nashville: Abingdon, 1984.

——. *Wesleyan Theology: A Sourcebook*. Durham, NC: Labyrinth, 1984.

*Lindström, Harald. *Wesley and Sanctification: A Study in the Doctrine of Salvation*. London: Epworth, 1946.

*Maddox, Randy L. *Responsible Grace: John Wesley's Practical Theology*. Nashville: Kingswood Books, 1994.

*Oden, Thomas C. *John Wesley's Scriptural Christianity: A Plain Exposition of His Teaching on Christian Doctrine*. Grand Rapids: Zondervan, 1994.

*Outler, Albert C., ed. *John Wesley*. New York: Oxford University, 1964.

*Thorsen, Don. *The Wesleyan Quadrilateral: Scripture, Tradition, Reason & Experience as a Model of Evangelical Theology*. Grand Rapids: Zondervan, 1990.

Wiley, H. Orton. *Christian Theology*. 3 vols. Kansas City: Beacon Hill, 1952-1953.

Williams, Colin W. *John Wesley's Theology Today*. New York: Abingdon, 1960.

Wynkoop, Mildred B. *Foundations of Wesleyan-Arminian Theology*. Kansas City: Beacon Hill, 1967.

*——. *A Theology of Love: The Dynamics of Wesleyanism*. Kansas City: Beacon Hill, 1972.

Roman Catholic Theology

(see also Vatican II)

*Broderick, Robert C. *The Catholic Encyclopedia*. Rev. ed. Nashville: Thomas Nelson, 1987.

Congar, Yves. *Diversity and Communion*. Mystic, CT: Twenty-Third Publications, 1985.

Cunningham, Lawrence. *The Catholic Experience: Space, Time, Silence, Prayer, Sacrament, Story, Person, Catholicity, Community, and Expectations*. New York: Crossroad, 1985.

——. *The Catholic Faith: An Introduction*. New York: Paulist, 1987.

Daly, Gabriel. *Transcendence and Immanence: A Study in Catholic Modernism and Integralism*. New York: Oxford University Press, 1980.

*Dulles, Avery. *The Reshaping of Catholicism*. San Francisco: Harper & Row, 1988.

Happel, Stephen, and David Tracy. *A Catholic Vision*. Philadelphia: Fortress, 1984.

*Hellwig, Monika K. *Understanding Catholicism*. New York: Paulist, 1981.

Hennesey, James J. *American Catholics: A History of the Roman Catholic Community in the United States.* New York: Oxford University Press, 1981.

Loome, Thomas M. *Liberal Catholicism, Reform Catholicism, Modernism: A Contribution to a New Orientation in Modernist Research.* Mainz: Matthias-Grünewald-Verlag, 1979.

*McBrien, Richard P. *Catholicism.* Rev. ed. San Francisco: HarperCollins, 1994.

*McBrien, Richard P., ed. *The HarperCollins Encyclopedia of Catholicism.* San Francisco: HarperSanFrancisco, 1995.

Nichols, Aidan. *The Shape of Catholic Theology: An Introduction to its Sources, Principles, and History.* Collegeville, MN: Liturgical Press, 1991.

*Rahner, Karl. *Foundations of Christian Faith.* New York: Seabury, 1978.

Ratzinger, Joseph. *The Ratzinger Report: An Exclusive Interview on the State of the Church.* San Francisco: Ignatius Press, 1985.

Ruether, Rosemary R. *Contemporary Roman Catholicism: Crises and Challenges.* Kansas City: Sheed and Ward, 1987.

Vidler, Alexander R. *A Variety of Catholic Modernists.* London: Cambridge University Press, 1970.

CONTEMPORARY THEOLOGICAL ISSUES

It is difficult to distinguish between what is a contemporary theological issue and what is of ongoing historic importance. Sometimes contemporary issues represent nothing more than ancient doctrines viewed in new and perhaps controversial ways. The following categories represent areas of theological study in which new insights have been brought to our attention. As such they represent special areas of concern to Christians today.

Arts

Balthasar, Hans Urs von. *The Glory of the Lord: A Theological Aesthetics.* 7 vols. Eds. Joseph Fessio and John Riches. San Francisco: Ignatius, 1983-1991.

Brown, Frank B. *Religious Aesthetics: A Theological Study of Making and Meaning.* New York: Macmillan, 1990.

Brown, Robert M. *Persuade Us to Rejoice: The Liberating Power of Fiction.* Louisville: Westminster/John Knox, 1992.

*Detweiler, Robert. *Breaking the Fall: Religious Readings of Contemporary Fiction.* Louisville: Westminster/John Knox, 1996.

Hyers, Conrad M. *The Comic Vision and the Christian Faith: A Celebration of Life and Laughter.* New York: Pilgrim, 1981.

——. *And God Created Laughter: The Bible as Divine Comedy.* Atlanta: John Knox, 1987.

Leeuw, Gerardus van der. *Sacred and Profane Beauty: The Holy in Art.* New York: Holt, Rinehart and Winston, 1963.

*Martin, Jr., James A. *Beauty and Holiness: The Dialogue Between Aesthetics and Religion.* Princeton: Princeton University Press, 1990.

*Wolterstorff, Nicholas. *Art in Action: Toward a Christian Aesthetic.* Grand Rapids: Eerdmans, 1980.

Asian Theology

Asia Theological Association. *The Bible and Theology in Asian Contexts: An Evangelical Perspective*. Taichung, Taiwan: Asia Theological Association, 1984.

Christian Conference of Asia, Commission on Theological Concerns. *Minjung Theology: People as the Subjects of History*. Rev. ed. Maryknoll, NY: Orbis, 1983.

England, John C. *Living Theology in Asia*. Maryknoll, NY: Orbis Books, 1981.

Fabella, Virginia, and Sun Ai Park Lee. *We Dare to Dream: Doing Theology As Asian Women*. Maryknoll, NY: Orbis Books, 1990.

Katoppo, Marianne. *Compassionate and Free: An Asian Woman's Theology*. Maryknoll, NY: Orbis Books, 1980.

*Lam, Wing-hung. *Chinese Theology in Construction*. South Pasadena: William Carey Library, 1983.

Lee, Jung Young. *The Trinity in Asian Perspective*. Nashville: Abingdon, 1996.

So, Kwang-son. *The Korean Minjung in Christ*. Hong Kong: Christian Conference of Asia, Commission on Theological Concerns, 1991.

Song, Choan-Seng. *Tell Us Our Names: Story Theology from an Asian Perspective*. Maryknoll, NY: Orbis Books, 1984.

*——. *Third-Eye Theology: Theology in Formation in Asian Settings*. Rev. ed. Maryknoll, NY: Orbis Books, 1991.

Black Theology

*Bailey, Randall C., and Jacquelyn Grant, eds. *The Recovery of Black Presence: An Interdisciplinary Exploration*. Nashville: Abingdon, 1995.

Boesak, Allan. *Black and Reformed*. Maryknoll, NY: Orbis Books, 1985.

Buswell III, J. Oliver. *Slavery, Segregation and Scripture*. Grand Rapids: Eerdmans, 1964.

*Cone, James H. *Black Theology and Black Power*. New York: Seabury, 1969.

——. *A Black Theology of Liberation*. Maryknoll, NY: Orbis Books, 1990.

*——. *God of the Oppressed*. New York: Seabury, 1975.

Jones, Major J. *Black Awareness: A Theology of Hope*. Nashville: Abingdon, 1971.

Jones, William R. *Is God a White Racist? A Preamble to Black Theology*. Garden City, NY: Anchor, 1973.

Keener, Craig S., and Glenn Usry, eds. *Black Man's Religion: Can Christianity Be Afrocentric*? Downers Grove: InterVarsity, 1996.

*King, Jr., Martin Luther. *I Have a Dream: Writings and Speeches that Changed the World*. San Francisco: HarperSanFrancisco, 1992.

*——. *A Testament of Hope: The Essential Writings of Martin Luther King, Jr*. San Francisco: Harper & Row, 1986.

Pannell, William. *The Coming Race Wars*? Grand Rapids: Zondervan, 1993.

Parratt, John. *Reinventing Christianity: African Theology Today*. Grand Rapids: Eerdmans, 1995.

Perry, Dwight. *Breaking Down the Barriers: A Black Evangelical Explains the Black Church*. Grand Rapids: Baker, 1996.

Reist, Benjamin A. *Theology in Red, White, and Black*. Philadelphia: Westminster, 1975.

*Roberts, J. Deotis. *Liberation and Reconciliation: A Black Theology*. Maryknoll, NY: Orbis Books, 1994.

*Shannon, David T., and Gayraud Wilmore, eds. *Black Witness to the Apostolic Faith*. Grand Rapids, Eerdmans, 1985.

*Skinner, Tom. *How Black Is the Gospel?* Philadelphia: Lippincott, 1970.

Smalley, Columbus, and Ronald Behm. *What Color Is Your God?* Downers Grove: InterVarsity, 1981.

Washington, Joseph. *Black Sects and Cults.* Garden City, NY: Doubleday, 1972.

Wilmore, Gayraud S. *Black Religion and Black Radicalism.* Maryknoll, NY: Orbis Books, 1983.

Wilmore, Gayraud S., and James H. Cone, eds. *Black Theology: A Documentary History, 1966-1979.* Maryknoll, NY: Orbis Books, 1979.

Charismatic Movement (see Pentecostal and Charismatic Theology)

Civil Religion

*Bellah, Robert N. *The Broken Covenant: American Civil Religion in Time of Trial.* Chicago: University of Chicago Press, 1992.

*Bellah, Robert N., and Phillip E. Hammond. *Varieties of Civil Religion.* San Francisco: Harper & Row, 1980.

Cuddihy, John M. *No Offense: Civil Religion and Protestant Taste.* New York: Seabury, 1978.

*Jones, Donald G., and Russell E. Richey, eds. *American Civil Religion.* New York: Harper & Row, 1974.

*Marty, Martin E. *A Nation of Behavers.* Chicago: University of Chicago Press, 1976.

Mead, Sidney E. *The Nation with the Soul of a Church.* New York: Harper & Row, 1975.

Neuhaus, Richard J. *Time Toward Home: The American Experiment as Revelation.* New York: Seabury, 1975.

*Pierard, Richard V., and Robert D. Linder. *Twilight of the Saints: Biblical Christianity and Civil Religion in America*. Downers Grove: InterVarsity, 1978.

Smith, Elwyn A. *The Religion of the Republic*. Philadelphia: Fortress, 1971.

Wilson, John F. *Public Religion in American Culture*. Philadelphia: Temple University Press, 1979.

Creation Science (See Creation)

Cross-Cultural Theology (Multicultural Issues)

(See also Culture)

Dyrness, William A. *Learning About Theology from the Third World*. Grand Rapids: Zondervan, 1990.

——. *Invitation to Cross-cultural Theology: Case Studies in Vernacular Theologies*. Grand Rapids: Zondervan, 1992.

*Dyrness, William A., ed. *Emerging Voices in Global Christian Theology*. Grand Rapids: Zondervan, 1994.

*Hesselgrave, David J. *Communicating Christ Cross-Culturally*. 2nd ed. Grand Rapids: Zondervan, 1991.

Kraft, Charles H. *Christianity in Culture: A Study in Dynamic Biblical Theologizing in Cross-Cultural Perspective*. Maryknoll, NY: Orbis Books, 1979.

Lee, Jung Young. *Marginality: The Key to Multicultural Theology*. Minneapolis: Fortress, 1995.

Russell, Letty M., et al. *Inheriting Our Mothers' Gardens: Feminist Theology in Third World Perspective*. Louisville: Westminster/John Knox, 1988.

Sittser, Gerald L. *Loving Across Our Differences*. Downers Grove: InterVarsity, 1994.

Smart, Ninian, and Steven Konstantine. *A Christian Systematic Theology in World Context*. Minneapolis: Fortress, 1991.

*Smith, Donald K. *Creating Understanding: A Handbook for Christian Communication Across Cultural Landscapes*. Grand Rapids: Zondervan, 1991.

Cults, New Age and the Occult

Boa, Kenneth. *Cults, World Religions and the Occult*. Wheaton, IL: Victor, 1990.

*Braaten, Carl E. *No Other Gospel!: Christianity Among the World's Religions*. Minneapolis: Fortress, 1992.

Braswell, Jr., George W. *Understanding Sectarian Groups in America*. Rev. ed. Nashville: Broadman & Holman, 1994.

Bromley, David G., and Anson D. Shupe, Jr. *Strange Gods: The Great American Cult Scare*. Boston: Beacon, 1981.

Chandler, Russell. *Understanding the New Age*. Grand Rapids: Zondervan, 1993.

Davies, Horton. *Christian Deviations*. Philadelphia: Westminster, 1973.

Ellwood, Jr., Robert S. *Religious and Spiritual Groups in Modern America*. Englewood Cliffs, NJ: Prentice-Hall, 1973.

Enroth, Ronald. *Churches That Abuse*. Grand Rapids: Zondervan, 1992.

——. *Recovering from Churches That Abuse*. Grand Rapids: Zondervan, 1994.

Groothuis, Douglas. *Confronting the New Age*. Downers Grove: Intervarsity, 1988.

——. *Unmasking the New Age*. Downers Grove: InterVarsity, 1986.

*Hexham, Irving, and Karla Poewe. *Understanding Cults and New Religions*. Grand Rapids: Eerdmans, 1986.

Hoekema, Anthony A. *The Four Major Cults*. Grand Rapids: Eerdmans, 1963.

Martin, Walter R. *The Kingdom of the Cults*. Grand Rapids: Zondervan, 1965.

*Mather, George, and Larry A. Nichols. *Dictionary of Cults, Sects, Religions and the Occult*. Grand Rapids: Zondervan, 1993.

Needleman, Jacob, and George Baker, eds. *Understanding the New Religions*. New York: Seabury, 1978.

*Tucker, Ruth A. *Another Gospel: Cults, Alternative Religions, and the New Age Movement*. Grand Rapids: Zondervan, 1989.

Culture

(See also Cross-Cultural Theology)

Jenson, Robert W. *Essays in Theology of Culture*. Grand Rapids: Eerdmans, 1995.

*Mayers, Marvin K. *Christianity Confronts Culture*. Rev. ed. Grand Rapids: Zondervan, 1987.

*Niebuhr, H. Richard. *Christ and Culture*. New York: Harper & Row, 1956.

——. *Radical Monotheism and Western Culture*. Louisville: Westminster/John Knox, 1993.

*Pelikan, Jaroslav J. *Jesus Through the Centuries: His Place in the History of Culture*. New Haven, CN: Yale University Press, 1985.

*Stott, John R.W., and Robert T. Coote, eds. *Down to Earth: Studies in Christianity and Culture*. Grand Rapids: Eerdmans, 1980.

Tillich, Paul. *Theology of Culture*. New York: Oxford University Press, 1959.

Wilson, John F. *Public Religion in American Culture*. Philadelphia: Temple University Press, 1979.

——. *Religion in American Society: The Effective Presence*. Englewood Cliffs, NJ: Prentice-Hall, 1978.

Death of God Theology

Altizer, Thomas J.J. *The Gospel of Christian Atheism*. Phladelphia: Westminster, 1966.

*Altizer, Thomas J.J., and William Hamilton. *Radical Theology and the Death of God*. Indianapolis, IN: Bobbs-Merrill, 1966.

*Gundry, Stanley N., and Alan F. Johnson, eds. *Tensions in Contemporary Theology*. Chicago: Moody, 1979.

Hamilton, Kenneth. *God Is Dead: The Anatomy of a Slogan*. Grand Rapids: Eerdmans, 1966.

*Ice, Jackson L., and John J. Carey, eds. *The Death of God Debate*. Philadelphia: Westminster, 1967.

*Montgomery, John W. *The "Is God Dead?" Controversy*. Grand Rapids: Zondervan, 1966.

Ogletree, Thomas W. *The Death of God Controversy*. Nashville: Abingdon, 1966.

Van Buren, Paul M. *The Secular Meaning of the Gospel*. New York: Macmillan, 1963.

Vahanian, Gabriel. *No Other God*. New York: G. Braziller, 1966.

Deconstructionism

Altizer, Thomas J. J. *Deconstruction and Theology*. New York: Crossroad, 1982.

Culler, Jonathan. *On Deconstruction: Theory and Criticism After Structuralism*. Ithaca, NY: Cornell University Press, 1982.

Norris, Christopher. *Deconstruction, Theory and Practice*. New York: Methuen, 1982.

*Taylor, Mark C. *Deconstruction in Context*. Chicago: University of Chicago Press, 1986.

Ecology (See Nature and Ecology)

Economics

(See also Politics)

Goudzwaard, Bob, and Harry de Lange. *Beyond Poverty and Affluence: Toward an Economy of Care*. Grand Rapids: Eerdmans, 1995.

*Meeks, M. Douglas. *God the Economist: The Doctrine of God and Political Economy*. Minneapolis: Fortress, 1989.

*Reed, Gregory. *Economic Empowerment and the Church*. Grand Rapids: Zondervan, 1994.

Schlossberg, Herbert, et al., eds. *Christianity and Economics in the Post-Cold War Era*. Grand Rapids: Eerdmans, 1994.

Schneider, John. *Godly Materialism*. Downers Grove: InterVarsity, 1994.

Sobrino, Jon. *The True Church and the Poor*. Maryknoll, NY: Orbis Books, 1984.

Wuthnow, Robert, ed. *Rethinking Materialism: Perspectives on the Spiritual Dimension of Economic Behavior*. Grand Rapids: Eerdmans, 1995.

Ecumenism

Brown, Robert McAfee. *The Ecumenical Revolution*. Garden City, NY: Doubleday, 1967.

*Fackre, Gabriel. *Ecumenical Faith in Evangelical Perspective*. Grand Rapids: Eerdmans, 1993.

*Fey, Harold E., Stephen Neill and Ruth Rouse, eds. *A History of the Ecumenical Movement*. Philadelphia: Westminster, 1970.

Flesseman-van Leer, Ellen., ed. *The Bible: Its Authority and Interpretation in the Ecumenical Movement*. Geneva: World Council of Churches, 1980.

Goodall, Norman. *The Ecumenical Movement*. London: Oxford University Press, 1964.

Jenson, Robert W. *Unbaptized God: The Basic Flaw in Ecumenical Theology*. Minneapolis: Fortress, 1992.

Leeming, Bernard. *The Vatican Council and Christian Unity*. London: Darton, Longman & Todd, 1966.

Massey, James E. *Concerning Christian Unity*. Anderson, IN: Warner, 1979.

Moeller, Charles and Gérard Philips. *The Theology of Grace and the Oecumenical Movement*. London: Mowbray, 1961.

*Murch, James DeForest. *Cooperation Without Compromise: A History of the National Association of Evangelicals*. Grand Rapids: Eerdmans, 1956.

Sartory, Thomas. *The Ecumenical Movement and the Unity of the Church*. Westminster, MD: Newman, 1963.

Torrance, Thomas F. *Theology in Reconciliation*. Grand Rapids: Eerdmans, 1975.

Van der Bent, Ans J. *Major Studies and Themes in the Ecumencal Movement*. Geneva: World Council of Churches, 1981.

Visser't Hooft, W.A. *The Pressure of Our Common Calling*. Garden City, NY: Doubleday, 1959.

Empirical Theology

(See also Experience)

Frankenberry, Nancy. *Religion and Radical Empiricism*. Albany: State University of New York, 1987.

Klocker, Harry R. *God and the Empiricists*. Milwaukee: Bruce, 1968.

*Meland, Bernard E., ed. *The Future of Empirical Theology*. Chicago: University of Chicago Press, 1969.

Miller, Randolph C. *The American Spirit in Theology*. Philadelphia: United Church, 1974.

Evangelicalism

Allan, John. *The Evangelicals*. Grand Rapids: Baker, 1989.

Barth, Karl. *Evangelical Theology: An Introduction*. New York: Holt, Rinehart and Winston, 1963.

Bloesch, Donald G. *The Evangelical Renaissance*. Grand Rapids: Eerdmans, 1973.

——. *The Future of Evangelical Christianity*. Colorado Springs: Helmers & Howard, 1988.

Dayton, Donald W. *Discovering an Evangelical Heritage*. New York: Harper & Row, 1976.

*Dayton, Donald W. and Robert K. Johnston, eds. *The Variety of American Evangelicalism*. Knoxville: University of Tennessee Press, 1991.

Ellingsen, Mark. *The Evangelical Movement*. Minneapolis: Augsburg, 1988.

Henry, Carl F.H. *Evangelicals in Search of Identity*. Waco: Word Books, 1976.

Inch, Morris A. *The Evangelical Challenge*. Philadelphia: Westminster, 1978.

Jewett, Paul K. *God, Creation, and Revelation: A Neo-Evangelical Theology*. Grand Rapids: Eerdmans, 1991.

Johnston, Robert K. *Evangelicals at an Impasse: Biblical Authority in Practice*. Atlanta: John Knox, 1979.

Kantzer, Kenneth S., ed. *Evangelical Roots*. Nashville: T. Nelson, 1978.

*Kantzer, Kenneth S., and Stanley N. Gundry., eds. *Perspectives on Evangelical Theology*. Grand Rapids: Baker Book House, 1979.

*Lightner, Robert P. *Evangelical Theology: A Survey and Review*. Grand Rapids: Baker Book House, 1986.

*Marsden, George M. *Understanding Fundamentalism and Evangelicalism*. Grand Rapids: Eerdmans, 1991.

McGrath, Alister E. *A Passion for Truth: The Intellectual Coherence of Evangelicalism*. Downers Grove: InterVarsity, 1996.

——. *Evangelicalism and the Future of Christianity*. Downers Grove: InterVarsity, 1995.

*Noll, Mark A., and David F. Wells, eds. *Christian Faith and Practice in the Modern World*. Grand Rapids: Eerdmans, 1988.

Padilla, C. René, ed. *The New Face of Evangelicalism*. Downers Grove: InterVarsity, 1976.

Pinnock, Clark, and Delwin Brown. *Theological Crossfire: An Evangelical/Liberal Dialogue*. Grand Rapids: Zondervan, 1991.

Ramm, Bernard L. *The Evangelical Heritage*. Waco: Word Books, 1973.

Webber, Robert, and Donald G. Bloesch, eds. *The Orthodox Evangelicals*. Nashville: T. Nelson, 1978.

Wirt, Sherwood Eliot. *The Social Conscience of the Evangelical*. New York: Harper & Row, 1968.

Existentialism

*Blackham, Harold J. *Six Existentialist Thinkers*. London: Routledge & Kegan Paul, 1952.

Bultmann, Rudolf. *Existence and Faith*. London: Hodder and Stoughton, 1961.

*Macquarrie, John. *Existentialism*. Philadelphia: Westminster, 1973.

——. *Studies in Christian Existentialism*. London: SCM, 1965.

*Michalson, Carl, ed. *Christianity and the Existentialists*. New York: Scribner's, 1956.

Roberts, David E. *Existentialism and Religious Belief*. New York: Oxford University Press, 1959.

Tillich, Paul. *The Courage to Be*. New Haven: Yale University Press, 1952.

Experience

(See also Empirical Theology)

*Dillistone, Frederick W. *Religious Experience and Christian Faith*. London: SCM, 1981.

Edwards, Denis. *Human Experience of God*. New York: Paulist, 1983.

*Edwards, Jonathan. *Religious Affections: How Man's Will Affects His Character Before God*. Portland, OR: Multnomah, 1984.

*James, William. *The Varieties of Religious Experience*. New Hyde Park, NY: University Books, 1963.

Knox, Ronald A. *Enthusiasm*. Oxford: Clarendon, 1959.

Lewis, Hywel David. *Our Experience of God*. New York: Macmillan, 1960.

Otto, Rudolf. *The Idea of the Holy: An Inquiry into the Non-rational Factor in the Idea of the Divine and Its Relation to the Rational*. New York: Oxford University Press, 1958.

*Proudfoot, Wayne. *Religious Experience*. Berkeley: University of California Press, 1985.

Smart, Ninian. *The Religious Experience of Mankind*. New York: Scribner's, 1969.

Tillich, Paul. *Ultimate Concern*. New York: Harper & Row, 1965.

Feminist Theology

(See also Humanity-Gender and Sexuality, Women)

*Bloesch, Donald G. *Is the Bible Sexist?* Westchester, IL: Crossway Books, 1982.

Boldrey, Richard, and Joyce Boldrey. *Chauvinist or Feminist? Paul's View of Women*. Grand Rapids: Baker, 1976.

Brown, Joanne C., and Carole R. Bohn, eds. *Christianity, Patriarchy, and Abuse: A Feminist Critique*. New York: Pilgrim, 1989.

Carmody, Denise L. *Responses to 101 Questions About Feminism*. New York: Paulist, 1993.

Chopp, Rebecca S. *The Power to Speak: Feminism, Language, God*. New York: Crossroad, 1989.

Clark, Elizabeth, and Herbert Richardson. *Women and Religion: A Feminist Sourcebook of Christian Thought*. New York: Harper & Row, 1977.

Coll, Regina. *Christianity and Feminism in Conversation*. Mystic, CT: Twenty-Third Publications, 1994.

*Daly, Mary. *The Church and the Second Sex*. New York: Harper & Row, 1968.

——. *Beyond God the Father: Toward a Philosophy of Women's Liberation*. Boston: Beacon, 1973.

Fiorenza, Elisabeth S. *Bread Not Stone: The Challenge of Feminist Biblical Interpretation*. Boston: Beacon, 1984.

——. *In Memory of Her*. New York: Crossroad, 1983.

*LaCugna, Catherine M., ed. *Freeing Theology: The Essentials of Theology in Feminist Perspective*. San Francisco: HarperCollins, 1993.

*Loades, Ann, ed. *Feminist Theology: A Reader*. Louisville: Westminster/John Knox, 1990.

*Malcolm, Kari T. *Women at the Crossroads*. Downers Grove: InterVarsity, 1982.

*Martin, Francis. *The Feminist Question: Feminist Theology in the Light of Christian Tradition*. Grand Rapids: Eerdmans, 1994.

Mercadante, Linda. *From Hierarchy to Equality: I Corinthians 11:2-16*. Vancouver: Regent College, 1978.

*Ruether, Rosemary R. *Sexism and God-Talk: Toward a Feminist Theology*. Boston: Beacon, 1983.

——. *New Woman—New Earth: Sexist Ideologies and Human Liberation*. New York: Seabury, 1975.

Russell, Letty M., ed. *Feminist Interpretation of the Bible*. Philadelphia: Westminster, 1985.

*Russell, Letty M., and J. Shannon Clarkson, eds. *Dictionary of Feminist Theologies*. Louisville: Westminster/John Knox, 1996.

*Scanzoni, Letha D., and Nancy A. Hardesty. *All We're Meant to Be: Biblical Feminism for Today*. Grand Rapids: Eerdmans, 1992.

Fundamental Theology (Roman Catholic)

*Metz, Johannes B. *The Development of a Fundamental Theology*. Mahwah, NJ: Paulist, 1969.

——. *Faith in History and Society: Towards a Practical Fundamental Theology*. New York: Seabury, 1980.

*O'Collins, Gerald. *Fundamental Theology*. Mahwah, NJ: Paulist, 1981.

O'Meara, Thomas F. *Fundamentalism: A Catholic Perspective*. New York: Paulist, 1990.

Fundamentalism (Protestant)

Ammerman, Nancy T. *Bible Believers: Fundamentalists in the Modern World*. New Brunswick: Rutgers University Press, 1987.

*Barr, James. *Fundamentalism*. London: SCM, 1977.

Boone, Kathleen C. *The Bible Tells Them So: The Discourse of Protestant Fundamentalism*. Albany, NY: State University of New York Press, 1989.

*Falwell, Jerry, et al., eds. *The Fundamentalist Phenomenon: The Resurgence of Conservative Christianity*. Garden City, NY: Doubleday, 1981.

Furniss, Norman F. *The Fundamentalist Controversy, 1918-1931*. Hamden, CT: Archon Books, 1963.

Gasper, Louis. *The Fundamentalist Movement, 1930-1956*. The Hague: Mouton, 1963.

Henry, Carl F.H. *The Uneasy Conscience of Modern Fundamentalism.* Grand Rapids: Eerdmans, 1947.

Marsden, George M. *Fundamentalism and American Culture: The Shaping of Twentieth-Century Evangelicalism, 1870-1925.* New York: Oxford University Press, 1980.

*——. *Understanding Fundamentalism and Evangelicalism.* Grand Rapids: Eerdmans, 1991.

Marsden, George M., ed. *The Fundamentals.* New York: Garland, 1988.

*Marty, Martin E., and Scott Appleby. *Fundamentalisms Observed.* Chicago: University of Chicago Press, 1991.

Sandeen, Ernest R. *The Roots of Fundamentalism: British and American Millennarianism, 1800-1930.* Chicago: University of Chicago Press, 1970.

Schaeffer, Francis A. *The Complete Works of Francis A. Schaeffer.* Westchester, IL: Crossway, 1982.

Hispanic/Latino Theology

(See also Liberation Theology)

Ellacuria, Ignacio. *Freedom Made Flesh: The Mission of Christ and His Church.* Maryknoll, NY: Orbis Books, 1976.

Gibellini, Rosino, ed. *Frontiers of Theology in Latin America.* Maryknoll, NY: Orbis Books, 1979.

Goizueta, Roberto S., ed. *We Are a People! Initiatives in Hispanic American Theology.* Minneapolis: Augsburg Fortress, 1992.

González, Justo L. *Out of Every Tribe and Nation: Christian Theology at the Ethnic Roundtable.* Nashville: Abingdon, 1992.

*Isasi-Díaz, Ada María, and Fernando F. Segovia, eds. *Hispanic/Latino Theology: Challenge and Promise.* Minneapolis: Augsburg Fortress, 1996.

*Ortiz, Manuel. *The Hispanic Challenge*. Downers Grove: InterVarsity, 1993.

Villafañe, Eldin. *The Liberating Spirit: Toward an Hispanic American Pentecostal Social Ethic*. Lanham, MD: University Press of America, 1992.

History

*Berkhof, Hendrikus. *Christ the Meaning of History*. Richmond: John Knox, 1966.

Braaten, Carl E. *History and Hermeneutics*. Philadelphia: Westminster, 1966.

*Cullmann, Oscar. *Salvation in History*. London: SCM, 1967.

Gilkey, Langdon. *Reaping the Whirlwind: A Christian Interpretation of History*. New York: Seabury, 1976.

Harvey, Van A. *The Historian and the Believer*. New York: Macmillan, 1969.

Kaufman, Gordon D. *Systematic Theology: A Historicist Perspective*. New York: Scribner's, 1978.

Kirkpatrick, Frank G. *Together Bound: God, History, and the Religious Community*. New York: Oxford University Press, 1994.

Metz, Johannes B. *Faith in History and Society*. New York: Seabury, 1980.

*Niebuhr, Reinhold. *Faith and History*. New York: C. Scribner's, 1949.

*Pannenberg, Wolfhart, ed. *Revelation as History*. New York: Macmillan, 1968.

Robinson, James M., and John B. Cobb, Jr., eds. *Theology as History*. New York: Harper & Row, 1967.

*Sykes, Stephen W., and John P. Clayton, eds. *Christ, Faith and History*. London: Cambridge University Press, 1972.

Vermes, Geza. *Jesus the Jew: A Historian's Reading of the Gospel*. 2nd ed. New York: Macmillan, 1983.

Wood, Herbert G., et al. *The Kingdom of God and History*. New York: Willett, Clark & Company, 1938.

Homosexuality

*Abelove, Henry, et al., eds. *The Lesbian and Gay Studies Reader*. New York: Routledge, 1993.

Brawley, Robert L. *Biblical Ethics and Homosexuality: Listening to Scripture*. Louisville: Westminster/John Knox, 1996.

Fuss, Diana, ed. *Inside/Out: Lesbian Theories, Gay Theories*. New York: Routledge, 1991.

McDonald, Helen B. *A Practical Guide to Counseling Lesbians, Gay Men, and Their Families*. New York: Continuum, 1990.

Satinover, Jeffrey. *Homosexuality and the Politics of Truth*. Grand Rapids: Baker, 1996.

*Schmidt, Thomas E. *Straight and Narrow?: Compassion and Clarity in the Homosexuality Debate*. Downers Grove: InterVarsity, 1995.

*Siker, Jeffrey S., ed. *Homosexuality in the Church: Both Sides of the Debate*. Louisville: Westminster/John Knox, 1994.

Humanism

Bouyer, Louis. *Christian Humanism*. London: G. Chapman, 1958.

d'Arcy, Martin C. *Humanism and Christianity*. New York: World Publishing, 1969.

Harbison, Elmore H. *The Christian Scholar in the Age of the Reformation.* New York: Scribner's, 1956.

Hitchcock, James. *What is Secular Humanism*? Ann Arbor: Servant, 1982.

Maritain, Jacques. *True Humanism.* London: Centenary, 1946.

*Packer, James I. *Christianity: The True Humanism.* Waco, TX: Word Books, 1985.

*Webber, Robert. *Secular Humanism: Threat and Challenge.* Grand Rapids: Zondervan, 1982.

Language, Religious

Caird, George B. *The Language and Imagery of the Bible.* Philadelphia: Westminster, 1980.

Charlesworth, Maxwell J. *The Problem of Religious Language.* Englewood Cliffs, NJ: Prentice-Hall, 1974.

Donovan, Peter. *Religious Language.* London: Sheldon, 1976.

*Gill, Jerry H. "The Meaning of Religious Language." *Readings in Christian Theology, Vol. 1.* Ed. Millard J. Erickson. Grand Rapids: Baker, 1973. Pp. 105-13.

*Hardesty, Nancy A. *Inclusive Language in the Church.* Atlanta: John Knox, 1987.

Macquarrie, John. *God-Talk.* New York: Harper & Row, 1967.

Mascall, E.L. *Words and Images.* New York: Ronald, 1957.

McFague, Sallie. *Metaphorical Theology: Models of God in Religious Language.* Philadelphia: Fortress Press, 1983.

——. *Speaking in Parables: A Study in Metaphor and Theology.* Philadelphia: Fortress, 1975.

*Ramsey, Ian T. *Religious Language*. London: SCM, 1957.

Ricoeur, Paul. *The Rule of Metaphor: Multi-disciplinary Studies of the Creation of Meaning in Language*. Buffalo: University of Toronto Press, 1977.

*Ruether, Rosemary R. *Sexism and God-Talk: Toward a Feminist Theology*. Boston: Beacon, 1993.

Soskice, Janet Martin. *Metaphor and Religious Language*. New York: Oxford University Press, 1985.

Liberal Protestantism (Modernism)

Cauthen, Kenneth. *The Impact of American Religious Liberalism*. New York: Harper & Row, 1962.

*Coleman, Richard J. *Issues of Theological Conflict: Evangelicals and Liberals*. Grand Rapids: Eerdmans, 1980.

*Dillenberger, John and Claude Welch. *Protestant Christianity Interpreted Through Its Development*. New York: Macmillan, 1988.

Hutchison, William R. *The Modernist Impulse in American Protestantism*. New York: Oxford University Press, 1982.

Mackintosh, H.R. *Types of Modern Theology*. London: Nisbet, 1937.

Miller, Donald E. *The Case for Liberal Christianity*. San Francisco: Harper & Row, 1981.

Parks, Leighton. *What is Modernism?* New York: C. Scribner's Sons, 1924.

*Pinnock, Clark, and Delwin Brown. *Theological Crossfire: An Evangelical/Liberal Dialogue*. Grand Rapids: Zondervan, 1991.

Reardon, Bernard M.G. *Liberal Protestantism*. Stanford, CA: Stanford University Press, 1968.

Liberation Theology

(See also Hispanic/Latino Theology)

*Armerding, Carl E., ed. *Evangelicals and Liberation*. Nutley, NJ: Presbyterian and Reformed Publishing, 1977.

Assmann, Hugo. *Theology for a Nomad Church*. Maryknoll, NY: Orbis Books, 1975.

Berryman, Philip. *Liberation Theology*. New York: Pantheon Books, 1987.

Boff, Leonardo, and Clodovis Boff. *Liberation Theology: From Confrontation to Dialogue*. San Francisco: Harper & Row, 1986.

Brown, Robert McAfee. *Theology in a New Key: Responding to Liberation Themes*. Philadelphia: Westminster, 1978.

Dussel, Enrique D. *History and the Theology of Liberation: A Latin American Perspective*. Maryknoll, NY: Orbis Books, 1976.

Eiesland, Nancy L. *The Disabled God: Toward a Liberatory Theology of Disability*. Nashville: Abingdon, 1994.

*Ellis, Marc H. and Otto Maduro, eds. *Expanding the View: Gustavo Gutiérrez and the Future of Liberation Theology*. Maryknoll, NY: Orbis Books, 1990.

*Gutiérrez, Gustavo. *A Theology of Liberation: History, Politics, and Salvation*. Maryknoll, NY: Orbis Books, 1973.

Hennelly, Alfred T. *Liberation Theology: A Documentary History*. Maryknoll, NY: Orbis Books, 1990.

Isasi-Díaz, Ada María, and Yolanda Tarango. *Hispanic Women: Prophetic Voice in the Church: Toward a Hispanic Women's Liberation Theology*. San Francisco: Harper & Row, 1988.

*Kirk, J. Andrew. *Liberation Theology: An Evangelical View from the Third World*. Atlanta: John Knox, 1979.

McGovern, Arthur. *Liberation Theology and Its Critics*. Maryknoll, NY: Orbis Books, 1989.

Míguez-Bonino, José. *Doing Theology in a Revolutionary Situation*. Philadelphia: Fortress, 1975.

Miranda, José P. *Marx and the Bible*. Maryknoll, NY: Orbis Books, 1974.

Musto, Ronald G., ed. *Liberation Theologies: A Research Guide*. New York: Garland, 1991.

Núñez C., Emilio A. *Liberation Theology*. Chicago: Moody, 1985.

*Segundo, Juan L. *The Liberation of Theology*. Maryknoll, NY: Orbis Books, 1976.

Liturgical Renewal

(See also Liturgy)

Benoit, Jean D. *Liturgical Renewal*. London: SCM, 1958.

*Botte, Bernard. *From Silence to Participation: An Insider's View of Liturgical Renewal*. Washington, DC: Pastoral, 1988.

Bouyer, Louis. *Liturgical Piety*. Notre Dame: University of Notre Dame Press, 1955.

Hageman, Howard G. *Pulpit and Table*. Richmond: John Knox, 1962.

Schmemann, Alexander. *Introduction to Liturgical Theology*. Portland, ME: American Orthodox, 1966.

Modernism (See Liberal Protestantism)

Myth

Bartsch, H.W., ed. *Kerygma and Myth*. London: SPCK, 1953.

Bultmann, Rudolf K. *Jesus Christ and Mythology*. New York: Scribner's, 1958.

*Gaskell, George., ed. *Dictionary of Scripture and Myth*. New York: Dorset, 1988.

*Goulder, Michael D., ed. *Incarnation and Myth*. Grand Rapids: Eerdmans, 1979.

Jaspers, Karl. *Myth and Christianity: An Inquiry into the Possibility of Religion Without Myth*. New York: Press, 1958.

Mackey, James P. *Jesus the Man and the Myth*. London: SCM, 1979.

Malbon, Elizabeth S. *Narrative Space and Mythic Meaning in Mark*. San Francisco: Harper & Row, 1986.

*Marshall, I. Howard., ed. *New Testament Interpretation*. Grand Rapids: Eerdmans, 1977.

Narrative

Calloud, Jean. *Structural Analysis of Narrative*. Philadelphia: Fortress, 1976.

Frei, Hans W. *The Eclipse of Biblical Narrative*. New Haven: Yale University Press, 1974.

Frye, Northrup. *Anatomy of Criticism*. Princeton: Princeton University Press, 1957.

*Goldberg, Michael. *Theology and Narrative: A Critical Introduction*. Nashville: Abingdon, 1982.

Harvey, Anthony E., ed. *God Incarnate: Story and Belief*. London: SPCK, 1981.

*Hauerwas, Stanley, and L. Gregory Jones, eds. *Why Narrative? Readings in Narrative Theology*. Grand Rapids: Eerdmans, 1989.

Kermode, Frank. *The Genesis of Secrecy*. Cambridge, MA: Harvard University Press, 1979.

Lodahl, Michael. *The Story of God*. Kansas City: Beacon Hill, 1994.

Malbon, Elizabeth S. *Narrative Space and Mythic Meaning in Mark*. San Francisco: Harper & Row, 1986.

McFague, Sallie. *Metaphorical Theology: Models of God in Religious Language*. Philadelphia: Fortress, 1983.

Middleton, J. Richard, and Brian J. Walsh. *Truth Is Stranger Than It Used to Be*. Downers Grove: InterVarsity, 1995.

*Stroup, George W. *The Promise of Narrative Theology*. Atlanta: John Knox, 1984.

Nature and Ecology

*Basney, Lionel. *An Earth-Careful Way of Life*. Downers Grove: InterVarsity, 1944.

*Birch, Charles, et al. *Liberating Life: Contemporary Approaches to Ecological Theology*. Maryknoll, NY: Orbis, 1990.

——. *The Liberation of Life: From the Cell to the Community*. New York: Cambridge University Press, 1981.

McDonagh, Sean. *The Greening of the Church*. Maryknoll, NY: Orbis, 1990.

Merchant, Carolyn. *The Death of Nature: Women, Ecology, and the Scientific Revolution*. San Francisco: Harper & Row, 1980.

Ruether, Rosemary R. *New Woman—New Earth: Sexist Ideologies and Human Liberation*. New York: Seabury, 1975.

Santmire, H. Paul. *The Travail of Nature: The Ambiguous Ecological Promise of Christian Theology*. Philadelphia: Fortress, 1985.

*Van Dyke, Fred, et al. *Redeeming Creation: The Biblical Basis for Environmental Stewardship*. Downers Grove: InterVarsity, 1996.

Young, Richard A. *Healing the Earth*. Nashville: Broadman & Holman, 1994.

Neoorthodox Theology

Barth, Karl. *Church Dogmatics*. 4 vols in 13. New York: Scribner, 1936-1969.

*——. *The Word of God and the Word of Man*. Grand Rapids: Zondervan, 1935.

*Berkouwer, G.C. *A Half Century of Theology*. Grand Rapids: Eerdmans, 1977.

Brunner, Emil. *Dogmatics*. 3 vols. Philadelphia: Westminster, 1950-1962.

——. *The Theology of Crisis*. New York: C. Scribner's Sons, 1929.

Bultmann, Rudolf. *History and Eschatology*. Edinburgh: University Press, 1957.

*Hordern, William. *The Case for a New Reformation Theology*. Philadelphia: Westminster, 1959.

Klassen, A.J., ed. *A Bonhoeffer Legacy*. Grand Rapids: Eerdmans, 1981.

Niebuhr, Reinhold. *Faith and History*. New York: C. Scribner's, 1949.

——. *Reflections on the End of an Era*. New York: C. Scribner's, 1934.

*Robinson, James M., ed. *The Beginnings of Dialectic Theology*. Richmond: John Knox, 1968.

Peace

Clouse, Robert G., ed. *War: Four Christian Views*. Downers Grove: InterVarsity, 1981.

Gremillion, Joseph, ed. *The Gospel of Peace and Justice: Catholic Social Teaching Since Pope John*. Maryknoll, NY: Orbis Books, 1976.

Hauerwas, Stanley. *Against the Nations: War and Survival in Liberal Society*. Minneapolis: Winston, 1985.

*——. *The Peaceable Kingdom: A Primer in Christian Ethics*. Notre Dame: University of Notre Dame Press, 1983.

Miller, Marlin E., and Barbara N. Gingerich, eds. *The Church's Peace Witness*. Grand Rapids: Eerdmans, 1994.

Stone, Ronald H. *Christian Realism and Peacemaking*. Nashville: Abingdon, 1988.

*Villafañe, Eldin. *Seek the Peace of the City: Reflections on Urban Ministry*. Grand Rapids: Eerdmans, 1995.

Will, James E. *A Christology of Peace*. Louisville: Westminster/John Knox, 1989.

——. *The Universal God: Justice, Love, and Peace in the Global Village*. Louisville: Westminster/John Knox, 1994.

*Wolterstorff, Nicholas. *Until Justice and Peace Embrace*. Grand Rapids: Eerdmans, 1984.

*Yoder, John Howard. *The Politics of Jesus*. Grand Rapids: Eerdmans, 1993.

Pluralism

Cobb, Jr., John B. *Christ in a Pluralistic Age*. Philadelphia: Westminster, 1975.

*Gaede, Stanley D. *When Tolerance Is No Virtue*. Downers Grove: InterVarsity, 1993.

Hick, John. *God and the Universe of Faiths*. London: Macmillan, 1973.

Hick, John, and Paul F. Knitter, eds. *The Myth of Christian Uniqueness: Toward a Pluralistic Theology of Religions*. Maryknoll, NY: Orbis Books, 1987.

Tracy, David. *The Analogical Imagination: Christian Theology and the Culture of Pluralism*. New York: Crossroad, 1981.

——. *Blessed Rage for Order: The New Pluralism in Theology*. New York: Seabury, 1975.

——. *Plurality and Ambiguity: Hermeneutics, Religion, Hope*. San Francisco: Harper & Row, 1987.

*Tracy, David, and John B. Cobb, Jr. *Talking About God: Doing Theology in the Context of Modern Pluralism*. New York: Seabury, 1983.

*Walls, Jerry L. *The Problem of Pluralism*. Wilmore, KY: Good News Books, 1986.

Politics

(See also Economics)

Borg, Marcus. *Conflict, Holiness and Politics in the Teachings of Jesus*. Lewiston, NY: Mellen, 1984.

Cobb, Jr., John B. *Process Theology As Political Theology*. Philadelphia: Westminster, 1982.

Cromartie, Michael, ed. *Caesar's Coin Revisited: Christians and the Limits of Government*. Grand Rapids: Eerdmans, 1996.

*Ellul, Jacques. *The Politics of God and the Politics of Man*. Grand Rapids: Eerdmans, 1972.

Fierro, Alfredo. *The Militant Gospel: A Critical Introduction to Political Theologies*. Maryknoll, NY: Orbis Books, 1977.

*Gutiérrez, Gustavo. *A Theology of Liberation: History, Politics, and Salvation*. Maryknoll, NY: Orbis Books, 1973.

Hill, Samuel S., and Dennis E. Owen. *The New Religious/Political Right in America*. Nashville: Abingdon, 1982.

Hinchliff, Peter. *Holiness and Politics*. Grand Rapids: Eerdmans, 1982.

Kee, Alistair. *A Reader in Political Theology*. Philadelphia: Westminster, 1974.

——. *The Scope of Political Theology*. London: SCM, 1978.

Míguez-Bonino, José. *Doing Theology in a Revolutionary Situation*. Philadelphia: Fortress, 1975.

Moltmann, Jürgen. *Religion, Revolution, and the Future*. New York: Scribner's, 1969.

*——. *On Human Dignity: Political Theology and Ethics*. Philadelphia: Fortress, 1984.

*Mouw, Richard J. *Politics and the Biblical Drama*. Grand Rapids: Eerdmans, 1976.

Norman, Edward R. *Christianity and the World Order*. New York: Oxford University Press, 1979.

Roberts, J. Deotis. *The Prophethood of Black Believers: An African American Political Theology for Ministry*. Louisville: Westminster/John Knox, 1994.

Soelle, Dorothee. *Political Theology*. Philadelphia: Fortress, 1974.

*Yoder, John Howard. *The Politics of Jesus*. Grand Rapids: Eerdmans, 1972.

Postmodernism

*Allen, Diogenes. *Christian Belief in a Postmodern World: The Full Wealth of Conviction*. Louisville: Westminster/John Knox, 1989.

*Anderson, Walter T. *The Truth about Truth: De-confusing and Re-constructing the Postmodern World*. New York: Putnam, 1995.

*Dockery, David S., ed. *The Challenge of Postmodernism: An Evangelical Engagement*. Wheaton: BridgePoint, 1995.

*Gill, Jerry H. *Mediated Transcendence: A Postmodern Reflection*. Macon, GA: Mercer University, 1989.

Grenz, Stanley J. *A Primer on Postmodernism*. Grand Rapids: Eerdmans, 1995.

Griffin, David R. *God and Religion in the Postmodern World*. Albany: State University of New York Press, 1989.

——. *Primordial Truth and Postmodern Theoogy*. Albany: State University of New York Press, 1989.

*——. *Varieties of Postmodern Theology*. Albany: State University of New York Press, 1989.

*Hauerwas, Stanley, et al., eds. *Theology Without Foundations: Religious Practice and the Future of Theological Truth*. Nashville: Abingdon, 1994.

*Lindbeck, George A. *The Nature of Doctrine: Religion and Theology in a Post-liberal Age*. Philadelphia: Westminster, 1984.

*Oden, Thomas C. *After Modernity...What?: Agenda for Theology*. Grand Rapids: Academie, 1990.

Taylor, Mark C. *Erring: A Postmodern A/Theology*. Chicago: University of Chicago Press, 1984.

Process Theology

Cargas, Harry James and Bernard Lee, eds. *Religious Experience and Process Theology: The Pastoral Implications of a Major Modern Movement*. New York: Paulist, 1976.

Cobb, Jr., John B. *God and the World*. Philadelphia: Westminster, 1969.

*Cobb, Jr., John B. and David R. Griffin. *Process Theology: An Introductory Exposition*. Philadelphia: Westminster, 1976.

Ford, Lewis S. *The Lure of God*. Philadelphia: Fortress, 1978.

Griffin, David R. *A Process Christology*. Philadelphia: Westminster, 1973.

Hartshorne, Charles. *Creative Synthesis and Philosophic Method*. London: SCM, 1970.

——. *The Divine Relativity: A Social Conception of God*. New Haven: Yale University Press, 1948.

*——. *Man's Vision of God and the Logic of Theism*. Hamden, CT: Archon, 1964.

*Nash, Ronald H. *Process Theology*. Grand Rapids: Baker, 1987.

Ogden, Schubert M. *The Reality of God*. New York: Harper & Row, 1966.

Pittenger, W. Norman. *Process Thought and Christian Faith*. New York: Macmillan, 1968.

Sia, Santiago. *God in Process Thought*. Dordecht, Netherlands: M. Nijhoff, 1985.

*Suchocki, Marjorie Hewitt. *God-Christ-Church: A Practical Guide to Process Theology*. New York: Crossroad, 1989.

Whitehead, Alfred North. *Religion in the Making*. New York: Macmillan, 1926.

Psychology of Religion

Argyle, Michael, and Benjamin Beit-Hallahmi. *The Social Psychology of Religion*. Boston: Routledge & K. Paul, 1975.

Boisen, Anton T. *The Exploration of the Inner World*. New York: Harper & Row, 1962.

Brown, Lawrence B. *Psychology and Religion*. Harmondsworth: Penguin Education, 1973.

Brown, Lawrence B., ed. *Advances in the Psychology of Religion*. New York: Pergamon, 1985.

*Carter, John D., and Bruce Narramore. *The Integration of Psychology and Theology*. Grand Rapids: Zondervan, 1979.

Donaldson, William J., ed. *Research in Mental Health and Religious Behavior*. Atlanta: Psychological Studies Institute, 1976.

Faber, Heije. *Psychology of Religion*. Philadelphia: Westminster, 1976.

Farnsworth, Kirk E. *Integrating Psychology and Theology*. Washington, DC: University of America, 1981.

*James, William. *Varieties of Religious Experience*. Ed. M.E. Harry. New Hyde Park, NY: University Books, 1963.

*Malony, H. Newton, ed. *Current Perspectives in the Psychology of Religion*. Grand Rapids: Eerdmans, 1977.

Myers, D.C., and M.A. Jeeves. *Psychology Through the Eyes of Faith*. Washington, DC: Christian College Coalition, 1987.

Otto, Rudolf. *The Idea of the Holy: An Inquiry into the Non-rational Factor in the Idea of the Divine and Its Relation to the Rational*. New York: Oxford University Press, 1958.

——. *The Mind Possessed*. Philadelphia: Lippincott, 1973.

Strunk, Orlo. *Mature Religion: A Psychological Study*. New York: Abingdon, 1965.

Thouless, Robert H. *An Introduction to the Psychology of Religion*. London: Cambridge University, 1971.

Tisdale, John R. *Growing Edges in the Psychology of Religion*. Chicago: Nelson-Hall, 1980.

Wulff, David M. *Psychology of Religion: Classic and Contemporary Views*. New York: Wiley, 1991.

Reason (Knowledge)

Brunner, Emil. *Revelation and Reason*. Philadelphia: Westminster, 1947.

*Davis, Stephen T. *Faith, Skepticism and Evidence: An Essay in Religious Epistemology*. Lewisburg: Bucknell University Press, 1978.

Hick, John. *Faith and Knowledge*. Ithaca, NY: Cornell University Press, 1966.

*Johnson, Phillip E. *Reason in the Balance*. Downers Grove: InterVarsity, 1995.

Mavrodes, George I. *Belief in God: A Study in the Epistemology of Religion*. New York: Random House, 1970.

Mavrodes, George I., ed. *The Rationality of Belief in God*. Englewood Cliffs, NJ: Prentice-Hall, 1970.

*Mitchell, Basil S. *The Justification of Religious Belief*. New York: Macmillan, 1973.

Penelhum, Terence. *Problems of Religious Knowledge*. New York: Herder and Herder, 1971.

*Swinburne, Richard. *Faith and Reason*. Oxford: Clarendon,1981.

*Torrance, Thomas F. *God and Rationality*. London: Oxford University Press, 1971.

Trigg, Roger. *Reason and Commitment*. Cambridge: University Press, 1973.

Ward, Keith. *Rational Theology and the Creativity of God*. Oxford: Basil Blackwell, 1982.

Science

Ferguson, Kitty. *The Fire in the Equations: Science, Religion, and the Search for God*. Grand Rapids: Eerdmans, 1995.

Giberson, Karl. *Worlds Apart: The Unholy War Between Religion and Science*. Kansas City: Beacon Hill, 1993.

Gilkey, Langdon. *Nature, Reality, and the Sacred: The Nexus of Science and Religion*. Minneapolis: Augsburg Fortress, 1993.

Hammond, Phillip E., ed. *The Sacred in a Secular Age: Toward Revision in the Scientific Study of Religion*. Berkeley: University of California Press, 1985.

Hooykass, Reijer. *Religion and the Rise of Modern Science*. Edinburgh: Scottish Academic, 1972.

Houghton, John T. *The Search for God: Can Science Help*? Oxford: Lion, 1995.

Jaki, Stanley, L. *Cosmos and Creator, Science and Creation*. Edinburgh: Scottish Academic, 1980.

——. *The Road of Science and the Ways to God*. Chicago: University of Chicago Press, 1978.

Klaaren, E. *Religious Origins of Modern Science*. Grand Rapids: Eerdmans, 1977.

Morris, Henry. *The Biblical Basis for Modern Science*. Grand Rapids: Baker, 1984.

*Pannenberg, Wolfhart. *Theology and the Philosophy of Science*. London: Darton, Longman & Todd, 1976.

*——. *Toward a Theology of Nature: Essays on Science and Faith*. Ed. Ted Peters. Louisville: Westminster/John Knox, 1993.

Peacocke, Arthur R. *Creation and the World of Science*. New York: Oxford University Press, 1979.

——. *Theology for a Scientific Age: Being and Becoming—Natural, Divine, and Human*. Minneapolis: Augsburg Fortress, 1993.

Polkinghorne, John. *Reason and Reality: The Relationship Between Science and Theology*. Philadelphia: Trinity Press International, 1991.

*Rae, Murray, et al., eds. *Science and Theology: Questions at the Interface*. Grand Rapids: Eerdmans, 1994.

*Torrance, Thomas F. *Divine and Contingent Order*. New York: Oxford University Press, 1981.

Secularity

*Alexander, John F. *The Secular Squeeze*. Downers Grove: InterVarsity, 1993.

*Ellul, Jacques. *The New Demons*. New York: Seabury, 1975.

Lyon, David. *The Steeple's Shadow: The Myths and Realities of Secularization*. Grand Rapids: Eerdmans, 1985.

*Oates, Wayne E. *Luck: A Secular Faith*. Louisville: Westminster/John Knox, 1995.

Smith, Ronald G. *Secular Christianity*. London: Collins, 1966.

Stark, Rodney, and William S. Bainbridge. *The Future of Religion: Secularization, Revival and Cult Formation*. Berkeley, CA: University of California Press, 1985.

Social Gospel

Abell, Aaron I. *American Catholicism and Social Action: A Search for Social Justice, 1865-1950*. Garden City, NY: Hanover House, 1960.

Carter, Paul Allen. *Decline and Revival of the Social Gospel*. Ithaca, NY: Cornell University Press, 1956.

Hopkins, Howard C. *The Rise of the Social Gospel in American Protestantism, 1865-1915*. New Haven, CT: Yale University Press, 1940.

Magnuson, Norris A. *Salvation in the Slums: Evangelical Social Work, 1865-1920*. Metuchen, NJ: Scarecrow, 1977.

May, Henry F. *Protestant Churches and Industrial America*. New York: Harper & Row, 1949.

*Niebuhr, H. Richard. *The Kingdom of God in America*. New York: Harper & Row, 1959.

Rauschenbusch, Walter. *Christianity and the Social Crisis*. 1907 rpt.; Louisville: Westminster/John Knox, 1991.

*——. *A Theology for the Social Gospel*. New York: Macmillan, 1917.

——. *Walter Rauschenbusch: Selected Writings*. Ed. W.S. Hudson. New York: Paulist, 1984.

*Smith, Timothy L. *Revivalism and Social Reform*. Baltimore: Johns Hopkins University Press, 1980.

Visser't Hooft, W.A. *The Background of the Social Gospel in America*. St. Louis: Bethany, 1963.

*Walsh, Brian J., and J. Richard Middleton. *The Transforming Vision*. Downers Grove: InterVarsity, 1984.

White, Jr., Ronald C. and Charles H. Hopkins, eds. *The Social Gospel: Religion and Reform in Changing America*. Philadelphia: Temple University Press, 1976.

Sociology and Anthropology of Religion

Bellah, Robert N. *Beyond Belief*. New York: Harper & Row, 1970.

*Berger, Peter L. *The Sacred Canopy*. Garden City, NY: Doubleday, 1967.

Boesak, Allan. *Farewell to Innocence: A Socio-Ethical Study on Black Theology and Black Power*. Maryknoll, NY: Orbis Books, 1977.

Bowker, John W. *The Sense of God: Sociological, Anthropological, and Psychological Approaches to the Origin of the Sense of God*. Oxford: Clarendon, 1973.

Eliade, Mircea. *The Sacred and the Profane: The Nature of Religion*. New York: Harcourt Brace, 1959.

*Ellul, Jacques. *The Subversion of Christianity*. Grand Rapids: Eerdmans, 1986.

Gill, Robin. *The Social Context of Theology*. London: Mowbrays, 1975.

——. *A Sociology of Religion*. New York: Basic Books, 1974.

——. *Theology and Social Structure*. London: Mowbrays,1977.

Grunlan, Stephen A., and Marvin K. Mayers. *Cultural Anthropology: A Christian Perspective*. Grand Rapids: Zondervan, 1988.

Lyon, David. *Christians & Sociology*. Downers Grove: InterVarsity, 1976.

Malina, Bruce J. *The New Testament World: Insights from Cultural Anthropology*. Louisville: Westminster/John Knox, 1993.

Martin, David. *The Religious and the Secular*. London: Routledge & K. Paul, 1969.

*Niebuhr, H. Richard. *Christ and Culture*. New York: Harper & Row, 1956.

*——. *The Social Sources of Denominationalism*. New York: H. Holt, 1929.

Robertson, Roland. *The Sociological Interpretation of Religion*. Oxford: Blackwell, 1970.

Scharf, Betty R. *The Sociological Study of Religion*. London: Hutchinson, 1970.

Towler, Robert. *Homo Religiosus*. London: Constable, 1974.

Troeltsch, Ernst. *The Social Teaching of the Christian Churches*. New York: Macmillan, 1931.

Walter, Julian A. *The Eclipse of Eternity: A Sociology of the Afterlife*. New York: St. Martin's, 1996.

Wilson, Brian R. *Contemporary Transformations of Religion*. New York: Oxford University Press, 1976.

——. *Religion in Sociological Perspective*. New York: Oxford University Press, 1982.

Tradition

*Anderson, George W., ed. *Tradition and Interpretation*. New York: Oxford University Press, 1979.

*Bruce, F.F. *Tradition, Old and New*. Grand Rapids: Zondervan, 1970.

Bruce, F.F., and E. Gordan Rupp, eds. *Holy Book and Holy Tradition*. Grand Rapids: Eerdmans, 1968.

Dillistone, Frederick W. *Scripture and Tradition*. London: Lutterworth, 1955.

Ebeling, Gerhard. *The Word of God and Tradition*. London: Collins, 1968.

Farmer, William R. *Jesus and the Gospel: Tradition, Scripture and Canon*. Philadelphia: Fortress, 1982.

Hanson, Richard P.C. *Tradition in the Early Church*. Philadelphia: Westminster, 1963.

Urban Issues

Abell, Aaron I. *The Urban Impact in American Protestantism*. Hamden, CT: Archon, 1962.

*Bakke, Ray. *The Urban Christian*. Downers Grove: InterVarsity, 1987.

Claerbaut, David. *Urban Ministry*. Grand Rapids: Zondervan, 1984.

Green, Clifford J., ed. *Churches, Cities, and Human Community: Urban Ministry in the United States, 1945-1985*. Grand Rapids: Eerdmans, 1996.

*Linthicum, Robert C. *City of God, City of Satan: A Biblical Theology for the Urban Church*. Grand Rapids: Zondervan, 1991.

*Villafañe, Eldin. *Seek the Peace of the City: Reflections on Urban Ministry*. Grand Rapids: Eerdmans, 1995.

Vatican II

Abbott, Walter M., and Joseph Gallaher, eds. *The Documents of Vatican II*. New York: Guild, 1966.

*Alberigo, Giuseppe, et al, eds. *The Reception of Vatican II*. Washington, DC: Catholic University Press of America Press, 1987.

*Hastings, Adrian, ed. *Modern Catholicism: Vatican II and After*. New York: Oxford University Press, 1991.

Miller, J.H., ed. *Vatican II: An Interfaith Appraisal*. Notre Dame: University of Notre Dame Press, 1966.

*Pennington, M. Basil. *Vatican II: We've Only Just Begun*. New York: Crossroad, 1994.

Vorgrimler, Herbert, ed. *Commentary on the Documents of Vatican II*. 5 vols. New York: Herder and Herder, 1967-69.

Violence

*Ellul, Jacques. *Violence: Reflections from a Christian Perspective*. New York: Seabury, 1969.

*Huber, Wolfgang. *Violence: The Unrelenting Assault on Human Dignity*. Minneapolis: Augsburg Fortress, 1996.

Hynson, Diana L., ed. *Violence*. Nashville: Abingdon, 1994.

*Kroeger, Catherine, and James R. Beck, eds. *Women, Abuse, and the Bible*. Grand Rapids: Baker, 1996.

Mayhew, Peter. *A Theology of Force and Violence*. London: SCM, 1989.

Merton, Thomas. *Faith and Violence: Christian Teaching and Christian Practice*. Notre Dame: University of Notre Dame, 1968.

Womanist Theology

Cannon, Katie G. *Black Womanist Ethics*. Atlanta: Scholars, 1988.

*Grant, Jacquelyn. *White Women's Christ and Black Women's Jesus: Feminist Christology and Womanist Response*. Atlanta: Scholars, 1989.

Grant, Jacquelyn, ed. *Perspectives on Womanist Theology*. Atlanta: ITC Press, 1995.

Townes, Emilie M. *In a Blaze of Glory*. Nashville: Abingdon, 1995.

Weems, Renita J. *Just a Sister Away: A Womanist Vision of Women's Relationships in the Bible*. San Diego: LuraMedia, 1988.

World Religions

Anderson, James N.D. *Christianity and World Religions*. Downers Grove: Inter-Varsity, 1984.

Braswell, Jr., George W. *Understanding World Religions*. Rev. ed. Nashville: Broadman & Holman, 1994.

*Clendenin, Daniel B. *Many Gods, Many Lords: Christianity Encounters World Religions*. Grand Rapids: Baker, 1995.

Hick, John. *God and the Universe of Faiths*. London: Macmillan, 1973.

Hick, John, and Paul Knitter, eds. *The Myth of Christian Uniqueness*. Maryknoll, NY: Orbis Books, 1987.

Lewis, James F., and William G. Travis. *Religious Traditions of the World*. Grand Rapids: Zondervan, 1991.

*Lyden, John, ed. *Enduring Issues in Religion*. San Diego: Greenhaven, 1995.

*Nash, Ronald H. *Is Jesus the Only Savior*? Grand Rapids: Zondervan, 1994.

*Neusner, Jacob, ed. *World Religions in America*. Louisville: Westminster/John Knox, 1994.

Parrinder, Geoffrey. *Avatar and Incarnation*. New York: Barnes & Noble, 1970.

*Pinnock, Clark H. *A Wideness in God's Mercy: The Finality of Jesus Christ in a World of Religions*. Grand Rapids: Zondervan, 1992.

Smith, W. Cantwell. *Towards a World Theology*. Philadelphia: Westminster, 1981.

APPENDIX

Writing and Publishing

*Gentz, William H., and Sandra H. Brooks. *Religious Writers Market-Place*. 4th ed. Nashville: Abingdon, 1993.

Goss, Leonard G., and Don M. Aycock, eds. *Inside Religious Publishing: A Look Behind the Scenes*. Grand Rapids: Zondervan, 1991.

*Hudson, Bob, and Shelley Townsend. *A Christian Writer's Manual of Style*. Grand Rapids: Zondervan, 1988.

*Miller, Donald E., and Barry J. Seltser. *Writing and Research in Religious Studies*. Englewood Cliffs, NJ: Prentice Hall, 1992.

*Stuart, Sally E. *Christian Writers' Market Guide*. Rev. ed. Wheaton, IL: Harold Shaw, 1996.

Taylor, John T. *A Manual of Bibliographical and Footnote Forms*. Ed. John L. Sayre. Enid, OK: Seminary, 1974.

INDEX